Sign Up Online

SBAC

Grade 5 Math Practice

Get Digital Access To

2 SBAC Practice Tests

5 Math Domains

Register Now

Url: www.lumoslearning.com/a/tedbooks

Access Code: SBACG5M-94078-P

SBAC Test Prep: 5th Grade Math Common Core Practice Book and Full-length Online Assessments: Smarter Balanced Study Guide with Performance Task (PT) and Computer Adaptive Testing (CAT)

Contributing Author - **April LoTempio**
Executive Producer - **Mukunda Krishnaswamy**
Designer and Illustrator - **Harini N.**

First Edition - 2020

NGA Center/CCSSO are the sole owners and developers of the Common Core State Standards, which does not sponsor or endorse this product. © Copyright 2010. National Governors Association Center for Best Practices and Council of Chief State School Officers.

SBAC is a copyright of The Regents of the University of California – Smarter Balanced Assessment Consortium., which does not sponsor or endorse this product.

ISBN-10: 1940484839

ISBN-13: 978-1-940484-83-9

Printed in the United States of America

Last updated - July 2022

For permissions and additional information contact us

Lumos Information Services, LLC
PO Box 1575, Piscataway, NJ 08855-1575
http://www.LumosLearning.com

Email: support@lumoslearning.com
Tel: (732) 384-0146
Fax: (866) 283-6471

Developed by Expert Teachers

INTRODUCTION

This book is specifically designed to improve student achievement on the Smarter Balanced Assessment Consortium (SBAC) Test. With over a decade of expertise in developing practice resources for standardized tests, Lumos Learning has designed the most efficient methodology to help students succeed on the state assessments (See Figure 1).

Lumos Smart Test Practice provides students SBAC assessment rehearsal along with an efficient pathway to overcome any standards proficiency gaps. Students perform at their best on standardized tests when they feel comfortable with the test content as well as the test format. Lumos online practice tests are meticulously designed to mirror the SBAC assessment. It adheres to the guidelines provided by the SBAC for the number of questions, standards, difficulty level, sessions, question types, and duration.

The process starts with students taking the online diagnostic assessment. This online diagnostic test will help assess students' proficiency levels in various standards.

After completion of the diagnostic assessment, students can take note of standards where they are not proficient. This step will help parents and educators in developing a targeted remedial study plan based on a student's proficiency gaps.

Once the targeted remedial study plan is in place, students can start practicing the lessons in this workbook that are focused on specific standards.

After the student completes the targeted remedial practice, the student should attempt the second online SBAC practice test. Record the proficiency levels in the second practice test to measure the student progress and identify any additional learning gaps. Further targeted practice can be planned to help students gain comprehensive skills mastery needed to ensure success on the state assessment.

Lumos Smart Test Prep Methodology

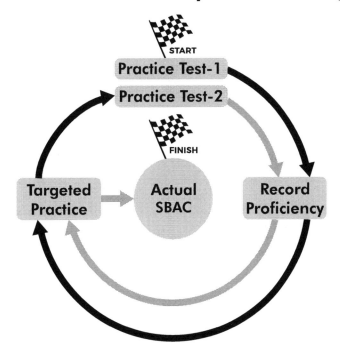

Figure 1

Table of Contents

Chapter 1
Lumos Smart Test Prep Methodology

Step 1: Access Online SBAC Practice Test

Use the URL and access code provided below or scan the QR code to access the first SBAC practice test to get started. The online SBAC practice test mirrors the actual Smarter Balanced assessments in number of questions, item types, test duration, test tools and more.

After completing the test, your student will receive immediate feedback with detailed reports on standards mastery. With this report, use the next section of the book to design a practice plan for your student.

URL	QR Code
Visit the URL below and place the book access code **www.lumoslearning.com/a/tedbooks** **Access Code: SBACG5M-94078-P**	

Step 2: Review the Personalized Study Plan Online

After student complete the online Practice Test 1, student can access their individualized study plan from the table of contents (Figure 2)
Parents and Teachers can also review the study plan through their Lumos account.

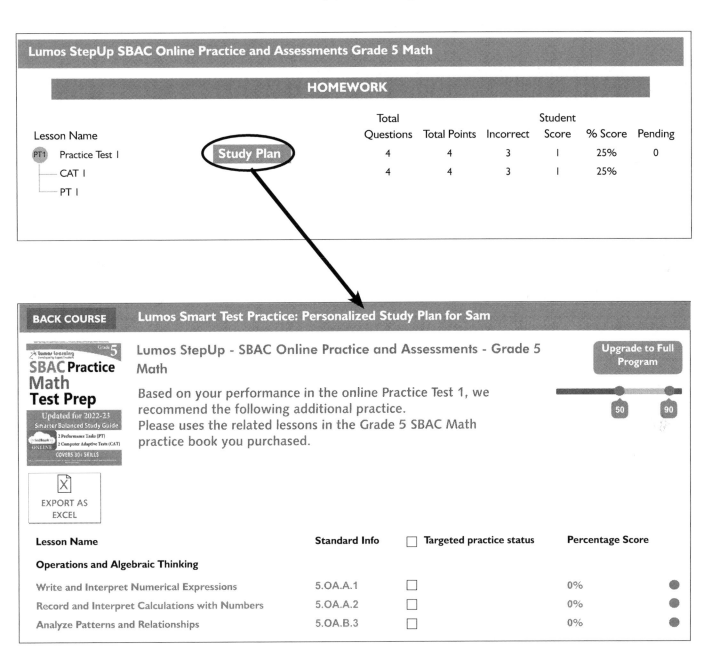

Lumos StepUp SBAC Online Practice and Assessments Grade 5 Math

HOMEWORK

Lesson Name		Total Questions	Total Points	Incorrect	Student Score	% Score	Pending
PT1 Practice Test I	Study Plan	4	4	3	I	25%	0
— CAT I		4	4	3	I	25%	
— PT I							

BACK COURSE   **Lumos Smart Test Practice: Personalized Study Plan for Sam**

Grade 5
SBAC Practice Math Test Prep
Updated for 2022-23
Smarter Balanced Study Guide
2 Performance Tasks (PT)
2 Computer Adaptive Tests (CAT)
ONLINE
COVERS 30+ SKILLS

Lumos StepUp - SBAC Online Practice and Assessments - Grade 5 Math

Based on your performance in the online Practice Test 1, we recommend the following additional practice.
Please uses the related lessons in the Grade 5 SBAC Math practice book you purchased.

Upgrade to Full Program

50   90

EXPORT AS EXCEL

Lesson Name	Standard Info	☐ Targeted practice status	Percentage Score	
Operations and Algebraic Thinking				
Write and Interpret Numerical Expressions	5.OA.A.1	☐	0%	●
Record and Interpret Calculations with Numbers	5.OA.A.2	☐	0%	●
Analyze Patterns and Relationships	5.OA.B.3	☐	0%	●

Step 3: Complete Targeted Practice

Using the information provided in the study plan report, complete the targeted practice using the appropriate lessons to overcome proficiency gaps. With lesson names included in the study plan, find the appropriate topics in this workbook and answer the questions provided. Students can refer to the answer key and detailed answers provided for each lesson to gain further understanding of the learning objective. Marking the completed lessons in the study plan after each practice session is recommended.(See Figure 3)

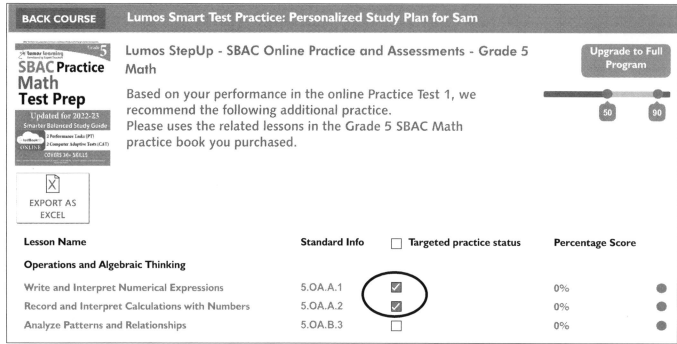

Figure 3

Step 4: Access the Practice Test 2 Online

After completing the targeted practice in this workbook, students should attempt the second SBAC practice test online. Using the student login name and password, login to the Lumos website to complete the second practice test.

Step 5: Repeat Targeted Practice

Repeat the targeted practice as per Step 3 using the second study plan report for Practice test 2 after completion of the second SBAC rehearsal.

Visit www.lumoslearning.com/a/lstp for more information on Lumos Smart Test Prep Methodology or Scan the QR Code

What if I buy more than one Lumos Study Program?

Step 1 → **Visit the URL given below and login to your account**

www.lumoslearning.com

Step 2 → **Click on 'My tedBooks' under the "Account" tab**

Place the Book Access Code and submit.

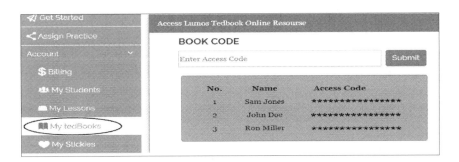

Step 3 → **Add the new book**

To add the new book for a registered student, choose the '**Existing Student**' button, select the student and submit.

To add the new book for a new student, choose the '**Add New Student**' button and complete the student registration.

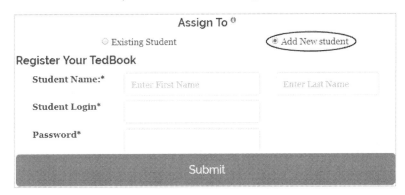

1) The day before the test, make sure you get a good night's sleep.

2) On the day of the test, be sure to eat a good hearty breakfast! Also, be sure to arrive at school on time.

3) During the test:

- **Read every question carefully.**

  - Do not spend too much time on any one question. Work steadily through all questions in the section.
  - Attempt all of the questions even if you are not sure of some answers.
  - If you run into a difficult question, eliminate as many choices as you can and then pick the best one from the remaining choices. Intelligent guessing will help you increase your score.
  - Also, mark the question so that if you have extra time, you can return to it after you reach the end of the section.
  - Some questions may refer to a graph, chart, or other kind of picture. Carefully review the graphic before answering the question.
  - Be sure to include explanations for your written responses and show all work.

- **While Answering Multiple-Choice (EBSR) questions.**

  - Select the bubble corresponding to your answer choice.
  - Read **all** of the answer choices, even if think you have found the correct answer.

- **While Answering TECR questions.**

  - Read the directions of each question. Some might ask you to drag something, others to select, and still others to highlight. Follow all instructions of the question (or questions if it is in multiple parts)

Chapter 2:
Operations and Algebraic Thinking

Lesson 1: Write and Interpret Numerical Expressions & Patterns

You can scan the QR code given below or use the url to access additional EdSearch resources including videos and mobile apps related to *Write and Interpret Numerical Expressions.*

 **Write and Interpret Numerical Expressions & Patterns**

URL	QR Code
http://www.lumoslearning.com/a/5oaa1	

1. Which of the following number sentences models the Associative Property of Multiplication? Circle the correct answer choice.

   Ⓐ 80 x 5 = (40 x 5) + (40 x 5)
   Ⓑ (11 x 6) x 7 = 11 x (6 x 7)
   Ⓒ 3 x 4 x 2 = 2 x 4 x 3
   Ⓓ 44 x 1 = 44

2. What is the value of 2 x [5-(6 ÷3)]?

3. Identify the expression that equals 2?

   Ⓐ [(3 x 2) + 4] ÷ 5
   Ⓑ 2 x [(5 x 4) ÷ 10]
   Ⓒ 12 - [(4 + 8) ÷ 3]

4. Rewrite the equation below, substituting a number value for 'a' and an operation for the question mark that would result in a solution of 10.
   20 ÷ [5 - (a ? 9)] = 10

5. Evaluate the expression (8 x 6) + (8 - 3)?

Ⓐ 53
Ⓑ 48
Ⓒ 64
Ⓓ 81

6. Where must the parentheses be in the following expression so that the answer is 6?
    20 - 8 ÷ 2

Ⓐ 20 - (8 ÷ 2)
Ⓑ (20 - 8) ÷ 2

7. Evaluate the expression 4 x (2 + 1) + 6.

Ⓐ 18
Ⓑ 15
Ⓒ 21
Ⓓ 16

8. In a drawing class, crayons were distributed to 12 students. Six of the students got packets that had 8 crayons and the other six got packets that had 10 crayons. How many crayons were distributed in all?

Ⓐ 110
Ⓑ 108
Ⓒ 100
Ⓓ 112

9. Jeremy had 20 books which he arranged in 4 shelves of a rack. His brother, Brandon takes away 4 books from each of the shelves. How many books are there now in each shelf?

Ⓐ 4
Ⓑ 5
Ⓒ 8
Ⓓ 1

10. Mary has 15 chocolates that she wants to put into packs of 3. She wants to give these packs to 4 of her friends. Choose the expression that fits the story.

Ⓐ (15 ÷ 3) + 4
Ⓑ (15 × 3) + 4
Ⓒ (15 × 3) − 4
Ⓓ (15 ÷ 3) − 4

Chapter 2

Lesson 2: Record and Interpret Calculations with Numbers

You can scan the QR code given below or use the url to access additional EdSearch resources including videos and mobile apps related to *Record and Interpret Calculations with Numbers*.

 **Record and Interpret Calculations with Numbers**

URL	QR Code
http://www.lumoslearning.com/a/5oaa2	

1. Which expression shows 10 more than the quotient of 72 divided by 8?

   Ⓐ $(10 + 72) \div 8$
   Ⓑ $(72 \div 8) + 10$
   Ⓒ $72 \div (8 + 10)$
   Ⓓ $8 \div (72 + 10)$

2. Which expression shows 75 minus the product of 12 and 4?

   Ⓐ $(75 - 12) \times 4$
   Ⓑ $(12 \times 4) - 75$
   Ⓒ $75 - (12 + 4)$
   Ⓓ $75 - (12 \times 4)$

3. Jamie purchased 10 cases of soda for a party. Each case holds 24 cans. He also purchased 3 packs of juice. Each pack of juice has 6 cans. Which expression represents the number of cans he purchased?

   Ⓐ $(10 \times 24) + (3 \times 6)$
   Ⓑ $(10 + 24) \times (3 + 6)$
   Ⓒ $10 \times (24 + 6)$
   Ⓓ $10 \times 24 \times 3 \times 6$

4. Olivia had 42 pieces of candy. She kept 9 pieces for herself and then divided the rest evenly among her three friends. Which expression best represents the number of candy each friend received?

   Ⓐ $(42 \div 3) - 9$
   Ⓑ $(42 - 9) \div 3$
   Ⓒ $42 \div (9 - 3)$
   Ⓓ $42 - (9 \div 3)$

5. Which is true about the solution to $8 \times (467 + 509)$?

   Ⓐ It is a number in the ten thousands.
   Ⓑ It is an odd number.
   Ⓒ It is eight times greater than the sum of 467 and 509.
   Ⓓ It is 509 more than the product of 8 and 467.

6. **Which is true about the solution to (3,259 – 741) ÷ 3?**

   Ⓐ It is one third as much as the difference between 3,259 and 741.
   Ⓑ It is 741 less than the quotient of 3,259 divided by 3.
   Ⓒ It is a whole number.
   Ⓓ It is a number in the thousands.

7. **Part A**
   Which of these expressions would result in the greatest number?

   Ⓐ 420 – (28 x 13)
   Ⓑ 420 + 28 + 13
   Ⓒ (420 – 28) x 13
   Ⓓ 420 + (28 x 13)

   Part B
   Which of these expressions would result in the smallest number?

   Ⓐ 684 – (47 + 6)
   Ⓑ 684 – 47 – 6
   Ⓒ (684 – 47) x 6
   Ⓓ 684 – (47 x 6)

8. **Each of the 25 students in a class sold 7 items for a fundraiser. Their teacher also sold 13 items. Which expression best represents the number of items they sold in all? Circle the correct answer choice**

   Ⓐ 25 x (7 + 13)
   Ⓑ 13 + (25 x 7)
   Ⓒ 7 x (25 + 13)
   Ⓓ 25 + 7 + 13

9. **Mario had $75. He doubled that amount by mowing his neighbor's lawn all summer. Then he spent $47 on new sneakers. Which expression best represents the amount of money he now has?**

   Ⓐ (75 x 2) - 47
   Ⓑ (75 + 75) ÷ 47
   Ⓒ 47 – (75 + 2)
   Ⓓ 75 + 2 - 47

Chapter 2

Lesson 3: Analyze Patterns and Relationships

You can scan the QR code given below or use the url to access additional EdSearch resources including videos and mobile apps related to *Analyze Patterns and Relationships*.

 **Analyze Patterns and Relationships**

URL	QR Code
http://www.lumoslearning.com/a/5oab3	

1. **Which set of numbers completes the function table?**
   Rule: multiply by 3

Input	Output
1	☐
2	☐
5	15
8	☐
12	☐

   Ⓐ 4, 5, 11, 15
   Ⓑ 3, 6, 24, 36
   Ⓒ 3, 6, 32, 48
   Ⓓ 11, 12, 18, 112

2. **Which set of numbers completes the function table?**
   Rule: add 4, then divide by 2

Input	Output
4	☐
6	☐
10	7
22	☐
40	☐

   Ⓐ 1, 3, 19, 37
   Ⓑ 10, 12, 28, 46
   Ⓒ 4, 5, 13, 22
   Ⓓ 16, 20, 52, 88

3. **Which set of coordinate pairs matches the function table?**
   Rule: multiply by 2, then subtract 1

Input	Output
5	☐
9	17
14	☐
25	☐

Ⓐ (5 , 9), (9 , 17), (14 , 27), (25 , 49)
Ⓑ (5 , 9), (14 , 25), (9 , 17), (27 , 49)
Ⓒ (5 , 9), (9 , 17), (17 , 14), (14 , 25)
Ⓓ (5 , 11), (9 , 17), (14 , 29), (25 , 51)

4. **Which set of coordinate pairs matches the function table?**
   Rule: divide by 3, then add 2

Input	Output
9	☐
15	7
27	☐
33	☐

Ⓐ (9 , 1), (15 , 7), (27 , 19), (33 , 25)
Ⓑ (9 , 5), (15 , 7), (27 , 11), (33 , 13)
Ⓒ (9 , 11), (15 , 7), (27 , 29), (33 , 35)
Ⓓ (9 , 15), (15 , 7), (7 , 27), (27 , 33)

5. Which set of numbers completes the function table?
   Rule: subtract 4

Input	Output
□	1
7	3
□	7
□	10
□	15

   Ⓐ 0, 3, 6, 11
   Ⓑ 3, 10, 17, 25
   Ⓒ 4, 28, 40, 60
   Ⓓ 5, 11, 14, 19

6. Which set of numbers completes the function table?
   Rule: add 1, then multiply by 5

Input	Output
□	5
2	15
□	20
□	35
□	55

   Ⓐ 2, 5, 15, 20
   Ⓑ 1, 4, 7, 11
   Ⓒ 30, 105, 180, 280
   Ⓓ 0, 3, 6, 10

7. Which rule describes the function table?

x	y
11	5
14	8
21	15
28	22

Ⓐ Add 3
Ⓑ Subtract 6
Ⓒ Subtract 1, then divide by 2
Ⓓ Divide by 2, Add 1

8. Which rule describes the function table?

x	y
4	4
7	10
13	22
20	36

Ⓐ Multiply by 2, then subtract 4
Ⓑ Add zero
Ⓒ Add 3
Ⓓ Subtract 1, then multiply by 2

9. **Which describes the graph of this function plotted on a coordinate grid?**

x	y
11	5
14	8
21	15
28	22

Ⓐ A curving line
Ⓑ A horizontal line
Ⓒ An upward sloping line
Ⓓ A downward sloping line

10. **Which type of function would result in a graph that looks like this?**

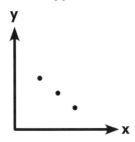

Ⓐ One in which x and y increase at fixed rates
Ⓑ One in which x and y decrease at fixed rates
Ⓒ One in which x decreases while y increases
Ⓓ One in which x increases while y decreases

11. **Consider the following two number sequences:**
    x: begin at 2, add 3
    y: begin at 4, add 6
    Which describes the relationship between the number sequences?

Ⓐ The terms in sequence y are two more than the terms in sequence x.
Ⓑ The terms in sequence y are six times the terms in sequence x.
Ⓒ The terms in sequence y are two times the terms in sequence x.
Ⓓ The terms in sequence y are half as much as the terms in sequence x.

12. Consider the following two number sequences:
    x: begin at 1, multiply by 2
    y: begin at 2, multiply by 2
    Which describes the relationship between the number sequences?

    Ⓐ The terms in sequence y are one more than the terms in sequence x.
    Ⓑ The terms in sequence y are two times the terms in sequence x.
    Ⓒ The terms in sequence y are two more than the terms in sequence x.
    Ⓓ The terms in sequence y are half as much as the terms in sequence x.

13. Consider the following number sequence:
    x: begin at 5, add 6
    Which would result in a relationship in which y is always three more than x?

    Ⓐ y: begin at 8, add 6
    Ⓑ y: begin at 5, add 9
    Ⓒ y: begin at 8, add 9
    Ⓓ y: begin at 2, add 6

14. Consider the following number sequence:
    x: begin at 4, multiply by 2
    Which would result in a relationship in which y is always half as much as x?

    Ⓐ y: begin at 4, multiply by 4
    Ⓑ y: begin at 4, multiply by ½
    Ⓒ y: begin at 2, multiply by 1
    Ⓓ y: begin at 2, multiply by 2

15. Use the table to answer the following question.
    What value of x would result in a y value of 16?

x	y
0	-2
3	7
4	10
9	25
12	34
10	38
5	13
	16

Ⓐ x = 6
Ⓑ x = 7
Ⓒ x = 8
Ⓓ x = 11

16. Consider the following pattern:
    7, 9, 4, 6, 1, . . .
    If the pattern continued, what would be the first negative number to appear?
    Write your answer in the box given below.

17. What is the next number in this pattern? Fill in the blank with the next number of the pattern.

    168, 152, 136, 120, _____

18. Kevin has been cutting lawns to earn some extra spending money. The first week he worked, he earned $10.00. Each successive week, for the next three weeks, he earned twice what he had earned the week before. How much money, in all, did he earn during the first four weeks of work? Write your answer along with the steps by which you ar rived at the answer in the box given below.

19. To find the next number in this pattern, multiply the term by 3 and then add 1.
    The first three terms in the pattern are 1, 4, and 13.
    What would the fifth term be? Circle the correct answer choice

    Ⓐ 121
    Ⓑ 120
    Ⓒ 129
    Ⓓ 111

End of Operations and Algebraic Thinking

Chapter 2:

Operations and Algebraic Thinking

Answer Key
&
Detailed Explanations

Lesson 1: Write and Interpret Numerical Expressions

Question No.	Answer	Detailed Explanations
1	B	The Associative Property of Multiplication states that when three or more numbers are multiplied, the product will be the same no matter how the three numbers are grouped. In this example, multiplying 11 x 6 x 7 will produce the same result whether the 11 x 6 are grouped together in parentheses or the 6 x 7 are grouped together. The other options are all mathematically correct, but they show different properties of multiplication.
2	6	When working with parentheses ( ) and brackets [ ], work from the inside to the outside. First solve the expression in the parentheses. 2 x [5 - (6 ÷ 3)] = 2 x [5 - (2)] Next solve the expression in the brackets. 2 x [5 - (2)] = 2 x [3] Finally, solve the resulting expression. 2 x [3] = 6
3	A	When working with parentheses ( ) and brackets [ ], work from the inside to the outside. [(3 x 2) + 4] ÷ 5 → [6 + 4] ÷ 5 → 10 ÷ 5 → 2 2 x [(5 x 4) ÷ 10] → 2 x [20 ÷ 10] → 2 x 2 → 4 12 - [(4 + 8) ÷ 3] → 12 - [12 ÷ 3] → 12 - 4 → 8
4		Think twenty divided by what is ten. Twenty divided by 2 is 10. Therefore two must equal what is in the brackets, 2=[5-(a ? 9)]. Next think, five minus what is two. Five minus three is two. Therefore three must equal what is in the parentheses, 3=(a ? 9). Now, we can get 3 by subtracting 9 from 12. 3=12-9 We can also divide 27 by 9 to get 3. 3 = 27 ÷ 9
5	A	First, evaluate the numbers within brackets 8 x 6 = 48 8 -3 = 5 Now, in step 2, add both the numbers. 48 + 5 = 53. Hence, A is the correct answer choice.
6	B	Choice A will be 20 - 4 = 16, while choice b is 12 ÷ 2 = 6. Hence, B is the correct answer choice.
7	A	4 x (2 + 1) + 6 = 4 x 3 + 6 = 12 + 6 = 18 Hence, answer choice A is correct.

Question No.	Answer	Detailed Explanations
8	B	$6 \times 8 = 48$ $6 \times 10 = 60$ $48 + 60 = 108$. Hence, answer choice B is correct.
9	D	The problem can be written as $(20 \div 4) - (1 \times 4)$ On solving, we get, $5 - 4 = 1$ Hence, answer choice D is the correct answer choice.
10	D	15 chocolates put into packs of 3 can be written as $(15 \div 3)$. She gives it to 4 of her friends. Hence, $(15 \div 3) - 4$ is the correct answer. Hence, D is the correct answer choice.

Lesson 2: Record and Interpret Calculations with Numbers

Question No.	Answer	Detailed Explanations
1	B	First, find the quotient of 72 divided by 8 (72 ÷ 8). Then determine what ten more than that would be (+ 10).
2	D	First, find the product of 12 and 4 (12 x 4). Then subtract the product from 75.
3	A	Show 10 cases of 24 as (10 x 24) and 3 six-packs as (3 x 6). Add the two expressions to find the total: (10 x 24) + (3 x 6).
4	B	First, subtract the 9 that Olivia kept for herself (42 – 9). Then divide the difference among the three friends: (42 – 9) ÷ 3.
5	C	The expression 8 x (467 + 509) indicates that you should first find the sum of 467 and 509, and then multiply by 8. Therefore, the solution is 8 times greater than that sum.
6	A	The expression (3,259 – 741) ÷ 3 indicates that you should first find the difference of 3,259 and 741, and then divide by 3. Therefore, the solution is one third as much as that difference.
7 Part A	C	A quick estimate shows that option C, a number in the hundreds times a number in the tens, would result in a number in the thousands. The other options would all result in a number in the hundreds.
7 Part B	D	A quick estimate shows that option D, in which the largest amount is subtracted from 684, would result in the smallest number. Options A and B subtract a relatively small amount from 684, and option C will actually result in a larger number.
8	B	First, multiply 7 items by the 25 students (25 x 7). Then add to that product the 13 the teacher sold: 13 + (25 x 7).
9	A	First, double the $75 he had (75 x 2). Then subtract the $47 he spent: (75 x 2) - 47.

Lesson 3: Analyze Patterns and Relationships

Question No.	Answer	Detailed Explanations
1	B	The rule is to multiply by 3, so plugging in each input number results in the following: 1 x 3 = 3, 2 x 3 = 6, 8 x 3 = 24, 12 x 3 = 36.
2	C	The rule is add 4, then divide by 2, so plugging in each input number results in the following: (4 + 4) ÷ 2 = 4, (6 + 4) ÷ 2 = 5, (22 + 4) ÷ 2 = 13, (40 + 4) ÷ 2 = 22.
3	A	The rule is multiply by 2, then subtract 1, so plugging in each input number results in the following: 5 x 2 - 1 = 9, 9 x 2 - 1 = 17, 14 x 2 - 1 = 27, 25 x 2 - 1 = 49. To create coordinate pairs, write the input number followed by the output number, separated by a comma, in parentheses.
4	B	The rule is divide by 3, then add 2, so plugging in each input number results in the following: 9 ÷ 3 + 2 = 5, 15 ÷ 3 + 2 = 7, 27 ÷ 3 + 2 = 11, 33 ÷ 3 + 2 = 13. To create coordinate pairs, write the input number followed by the output number, separated by a comma, in parentheses.
5	D	The rule is -4, Option (A) is incorrect. because 0 -4 = -4 and not 1. (If the rule does not work for one number, we need not check for other numbers). Option (B) is incorrect, because 3 - 4 = -1 and not 1. Option (C) is incorrect, because 4 - 4 = 0 and not 1. All the numbers in option (D) satisfy the rule. 5 – 4 = 1, 11 – 4 = 7, 14 – 4 = 10, 19 – 4 = 15
6	D	The rule is +1, x5, Option (A) is incorrect, because (2 + 1) x 5 = 15 not 5. (If the rule does not work for one number, we need not check for other numbers). Option (B) is incorrect, because (1 + 1) x 5 =10 not 5 Option (C) is incorrect, because (30 + 1) x 5 = 155 not 5 All the numbers in option (D) satisfies the rule. (0 + 1) x 5 = 5, (3 + 1) x 5 = 20, (6 + 1) x 5 = 35, (10 + 1) x 5 = 55.
7	B	Option (A) is incorrect, because 11 + 3 = 14 NOT 5. Option (B) is correct, as subtracting 6 from each x-value results in the corresponding y-value as follows: 11 – 6 = 5, 14 – 6 = 8, 21 – 6 = 15, 28 – 6 = 22. Note that, once we get the correct option, we need not check other options.

Question No.	Answer	Detailed Explanations
8	A	Option (A) is correct because multiplying each x-value by 2 and then subtracting 4 results in the corresponding y-value as follows: $4 \times 2 - 4 = 4$, $7 \times 2 - 4 = 10$, $13 \times 2 - 4 = 22$, $20 \times 2 - 4 = 36$. Note that, once we get the correct option, we need not check other options.
9	C	As the value of x increases, the value of y increases, both at fixed rates. This produces an upward-sloping straight line.
10	D	If the value of x increases while the value of y decreases, the function produces a downward sloping straight line.
11	C	According to the rules, sequence x would begin 2, 5, 8, ..., and sequence y would begin 4, 10, 16, ... Therefore, the terms in sequence y are always two times the terms in sequence x.
12	B	According to the rules, sequence x would begin 1, 2, 4, ..., and sequence y would begin 2, 4, 8, ... Therefore, the terms in sequence y are always two times the terms in sequence x.
13	A	Sequence x : 5, 11, 17, ... According to the rule in option A, sequence y : 8, 14, 20, ... Therefore, the terms in sequence y are always three more than the terms in sequence x. Option (A) is the Correct Answer. Note that, once we get the correct option, we need to check the other options.
14	D	Sequence x : 4, 8, 16,.... Sequence y in option (A) : 4, 16, 64 ..... comparing sequence x and sequence y, we see that given rule is NOT satisfied. So, option (A) is incorrect. Sequence y in option (B) : 4, 2, 1 .... comparing sequence x and sequence y, we see that given rule is NOT satisfied. So, option (B) is incorrect. Sequence y in option (C) : 2, 2, 2 ... comparing sequence x and sequence y, we see that given rule is NOT satisfied. So, option (C) is incorrect. Sequence y in option (D) : 2, 4, 8 .... comparing sequence x and sequence y, we see that terms in sequence y are always half as much as the terms in sequence x. So, option (D) is correct.
15	A	The numbers in the table follow the pattern 3x - 2 = y. By plugging in 16 for y, the equation becomes 3x - 2 = 16. Add 2 to each side of the equation to get 3x = 18. Divide each side of the equation by 3 to get x = 6.

Question No.	Answer	Detailed Explanations
16	-2	The pattern is Add 2, Subtract 5. Since 5 was just subtracted from 6 to get 1, the pattern would continue: 3, -2 . . .
17	104	Determine the pattern by solving for 168 - x = 152. Then check the result (x = 16) with another term in the pattern (152 - 16 = 136). Now apply the rule to the final term to determine which number comes next (120 - 16 = 104).
18		The first week, Kevin earned $10.00. The second week, he earned twice that, or $20.00. The third week, he earned twice that, or $40.00. The fourth week, he earned twice that, or $80.00. To find the total for all four weeks, add $10.00 + $20.00 + $40.00 + $80.00 to get a total of $150.00.
19	A	Continue the pattern "3x + 1" starting from 13: 3 (13) + 1 = 40 3 (40) + 1 = 121

Chapter 3:
Number & Operations in Base Ten

Lesson 1: Place Value

You can scan the QR code given below or use the url to access additional EdSearch resources including videos and mobile apps related to *Place Value*.

ed)Search   *Place Value*

URL	QR Code
http://www.lumoslearning.com/a/5nbta1	

1. **In the number 913,874 which digit is in the ten thousands place?**

    Ⓐ 8
    Ⓑ 1
    Ⓒ 9
    Ⓓ 3

2. **In the number 7.2065 which digit is in the thousandths place?**

    Ⓐ 5
    Ⓑ 2
    Ⓒ 0
    Ⓓ 6

3. **Which number is equivalent to 8/10?**

    Ⓐ 0.8
    Ⓑ 8.0
    Ⓒ 0.08
    Ⓓ 0.008

4. **What is the equivalent of 4 and 3/100?**

    Ⓐ 40.3
    Ⓑ 0.403
    Ⓒ 4.03
    Ⓓ 403.0

5. **In the number 16,428,095 what is the value of the digit 6?**

    Ⓐ 6 million
    Ⓑ 60 thousand
    Ⓒ 60 million
    Ⓓ 600 thousand

6. **What is the value of 9 in the number 5,802.109**

    Ⓐ 9 thousand
    Ⓑ 9 tenths
    Ⓒ 9 thousandths
    Ⓓ 9 hundredths

7. **Which comparison is correct?**

   Ⓐ 50.5 = 50.05
   Ⓑ 0.05 = 0.50
   Ⓒ 0.005 = 500.0
   Ⓓ 0.50 = 0.500

8. **Which number is one hundredth less than 406.51?**

   Ⓐ 406.41
   Ⓑ 406.50
   Ⓒ 306.51
   Ⓓ 406.01

9. **Which of the following numbers is greater than 8.4?**

   Ⓐ 8.41
   Ⓑ 8.40
   Ⓒ 8.14
   Ⓓ 8.04

10. **Which of the following numbers is less than 2.17?**

    Ⓐ 21.7
    Ⓑ 2.71
    Ⓒ 2.170
    Ⓓ 2.07

11. **When comparing 385.24 with 452.38 which of the following statements are correct? Select all that apply.**

    Ⓐ The digit 3 in 385.24 is 1000 times greater than the 3 in 452.38.
    Ⓑ The digit 5 is ten times less in 452.38 than in 385.24.
    Ⓒ The digit 8 is 100 times more in 385.24 than in 452.38.
    Ⓓ The digit 2 is 10 times more in 452.38 than in 385.24

12. Read each statement and indicate whether it is true or false.

	True	False
The 5 in 570.22 is ten times greater than 5 in 456.1	○	○
The 8 in 2.083 is hundred times less than the 8 in 328.7	○	○
The 3 in 1.039 is hundred times less than the 3 in 67.3	○	○
The 2 in 9,523 is thousand times more than the 2 in 45.92	○	○

13. Fill in the blank.

The place value of the digit 3 in 67.039 is _____.

14. The digit 7 in which of the following numbers is hundred times more than the 7 in 539.7? Circle the correct answer choice

Ⓐ 172.43
Ⓑ 2728.4
Ⓒ 7426.1
Ⓓ 65.907

Chapter 3

Lesson 2: Multiplication & Division of Powers of Ten

You can scan the QR code given below or use the url to access additional EdSearch resources including videos and mobile apps related to *Multiplication & Division of Powers of Ten*.

 Multiplication & Division of Powers of Ten

URL	QR Code
http://www.lumoslearning.com/a/5nbta2	

1. **Solve: $9 \times 10^3 =$**

    Ⓐ 900
    Ⓑ 9,000
    Ⓒ 117
    Ⓓ 270

2. **What is the quotient of 10^7 divided by 100?**

    Ⓐ 0.7
    Ⓑ 100,000
    Ⓒ 70,000
    Ⓓ 700

3. **Solve: 0.51 x _____ = 5,100**

    Ⓐ 10^4
    Ⓑ 10^2
    Ⓒ 100
    Ⓓ 10^3

4. **Astronomers calculate a distant star to be 3×10^5 light years away. How far away is the star?**

    Ⓐ 30,000 light years
    Ⓑ 3,000 light years
    Ⓒ 3,000,000 light years
    Ⓓ 300,000 light years

5. **A scientist calculates the weight of a substance as $6.9 \div 10^4$ grams. What is the weight of the substance?**

    Ⓐ 69,000 grams
    Ⓑ 69 milligrams
    Ⓒ 0.00069 grams
    Ⓓ 6.9 kilograms

6. **Looking through a microscope, a doctor finds a germ that is 0.00000082 millimeters long. How can he write this number in his notes?**

    Ⓐ 8.2×10^7
    Ⓑ $8.2 \div 10^7$
    Ⓒ $8.2 \times 10^{0.00001}$
    Ⓓ $8.2 \div 700$

7. Which of the following is 10^5 times greater than 0.016?

 Ⓐ 160
 Ⓑ 1,600
 Ⓒ 16.0
 Ⓓ 1.60

8. Find the missing number.
   _____ x 477 = 47,700,000

 Ⓐ 10,000,000
 Ⓑ 10 x 5
 Ⓒ 10^5
 Ⓓ 1,000

9. The number 113 is _____ times greater than 0.113.

 Ⓐ 3
 Ⓑ 10^3
 Ⓒ 30
 Ⓓ 10,000

10. _____ ÷ 10^5 = 4.6

 Ⓐ 460
 Ⓑ 4,600
 Ⓒ 46,000
 Ⓓ 460,000

11. Complete the table by writing the given number as a power of ten or the power of ten as a standard number.

1,000,000	
	10^4
100	
	10^7

12. Write the number 1,000 as a power of ten. Enter your answer in the box given below

13. Circle the power of ten that represents 100,000,000.

Ⓐ 10^6
Ⓑ 10^8
Ⓒ 10^9
Ⓓ 10^{10}

Chapter 3

Lesson 3: Read and Write Decimals

You can scan the QR code given below or use the url to access additional EdSearch resources including videos and mobile apps related to *Read and Write Decimals*.

 **Read and Write Decimals**

URL	QR Code
http://www.lumoslearning.com/a/5nbta3	

1. **How is the number four hundredths written?**

    Ⓐ 0.04
    Ⓑ 0.400
    Ⓒ 400.0
    Ⓓ 0.004

2. **How is the number 0.2 read?**

    Ⓐ Zero and two
    Ⓑ Decimal two
    Ⓒ Two tenths
    Ⓓ Two hundredths

3. **What is the decimal form of $\frac{7}{10}$?**

    Ⓐ 7.10
    Ⓑ 0.7
    Ⓒ 10.7
    Ⓓ 0.07

4. **The number 0.05 can be represented by which fraction?**

    Ⓐ $\frac{0}{5}$

    Ⓑ $\frac{5}{100}$

    Ⓒ $\frac{5}{10}$

    Ⓓ $\frac{1}{05}$

5. **Which of the following numbers is equivalent to one half?**

    Ⓐ 0.2
    Ⓑ 0.12
    Ⓒ 1.2
    Ⓓ 0.5

6. **How is the number sixty three hundredths written?**

    Ⓐ 0.63
    Ⓑ 0.063
    Ⓒ 0.0063
    Ⓓ 6.300

7. What is the correct way to read the number 40.057?

Ⓐ Forty point five seven
Ⓑ Forty and fifty-seven hundredths
Ⓒ Forty and fifty-seven thousandths
Ⓓ Forty and five hundredths and seven thousandths

8. Which of the following numbers has:
0 in the hundredths place
8 in the tenths place
3 in the thousandths place
9 in the ones place

Ⓐ 9.083
Ⓑ 0.839
Ⓒ 9.803
Ⓓ 0.9803

9. For which number is this the expanded form?
$9 \times 10 + 2 \times 1 + 3 \times (\frac{1}{10}) + 8 \times (\frac{1}{100})$

Ⓐ 98.08
Ⓑ 93.48
Ⓒ 9.238
Ⓓ 92.38

10. What is the correct expanded form of the number 0.85?

Ⓐ $(8 \times 10) + (5 \times 100)$
Ⓑ $8 \times (\frac{1}{10}) + 5 \times (\frac{1}{100})$
Ⓒ $85 \div 10$
Ⓓ $(8 \div 10) \times (5 \div 10)$

11. Which of the following numbers are written correctly in expanded form? Note that more than one option may be correct. Select all the correct answers

Ⓐ $452.25 = 4 \times 100 + 5 \times 10 + 2 \times 1 + 1 + 5 \times 10$
Ⓑ $53.81 = 5 \times 10 + 3 \times 1 + 8 \times (\frac{1}{10}) + 1 \times (\frac{1}{100})$
Ⓒ $3.72 = 3 \times 1 + 7 \times (\frac{10}{1}) + 2 \times (\frac{100}{1})$
Ⓓ $923.04 = 9 \times 100 + 2 \times 10 + 3 \times 1 + 4 \times (\frac{1}{100})$

12. Read the equations below and indicate whether they are true or false.

	True	False
345.3 = three hundred forty-five and three hundredths.	○	○
$900 \times 30 \times 2 \times 4 \times(\frac{1}{10}) \times 7(\frac{1}{100})$ > Nine hundred thirty-two and four hundredths	○	○
$604.2 = 600 \times 4 \times 2 \times (\frac{1}{100})$	○	○
1.805 > One and ninety-two hundredths	○	○

13. What is the standard form of this number?
    Seventy-nine million, four hundred seventeen thousand, six hundred eight
    Enter your answer in the box given below

14. Which of the following represents four thousand sixty-two and thirteen hundredths?
    Circle the correct answer choice.

    Ⓐ 462.13
    Ⓑ 4,602.013
    Ⓒ 4,062.13
    Ⓓ 4620.13

Chapter 3

Lesson 4: Comparing and Ordering Decimals

You can scan the QR code given below or use the url to access additional EdSearch resources including videos and mobile apps related to *Comparing and Ordering Decimals*.

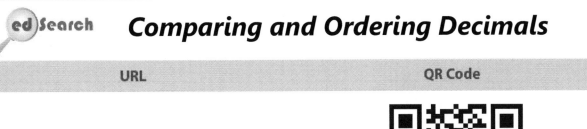

Comparing and Ordering Decimals

URL	QR Code
http://www.lumoslearning.com/a/5nbta3	

1. Which of the following numbers is the least?
   0.04, 4.00, 0.40, 40.0

   Ⓐ 0.04
   Ⓑ 4.00
   Ⓒ 0.40
   Ⓓ 40.0

2. Which of the following numbers is greatest?
   0.125, 0.251, 0.512, 0.215

   Ⓐ 0.125
   Ⓑ 0.251
   Ⓒ 0.512
   Ⓓ 0.215

3. Which of the following numbers is less than seven hundredths?

   Ⓐ 0.072
   Ⓑ 0.60
   Ⓒ 0.058
   Ⓓ All of these

4. Which of the following comparisons is correct?

   Ⓐ 48.01 = 48.1
   Ⓑ 25.4 < 25.40
   Ⓒ 10.83 < 10.093
   Ⓓ 392.01 < 392.1

5. Arrange these numbers in order from least to greatest:
   1.02, 1.2, 1.12, 2.12

   Ⓐ 1.2, 1.12, 1.02, 2.12
   Ⓑ 2.12, 1.2, 1.12, 1.02
   Ⓒ 1.02, 1.12, 1.2, 2.12
   Ⓓ 1.12, 2.12, 1.02, 1.2

6. Which of the following is true?

   Ⓐ 3.21 > 32.1
   Ⓑ 32.12 > 312.12
   Ⓒ 32.12 > 3.212
   Ⓓ 212.3 < 21.32

7. Arrange these numbers in order from greatest to least:
   2.4, 2.04, 2.21, 2.20

   Ⓐ 2.4, 2.04, 2.21, 2.20
   Ⓑ 2.4, 2.21, 2.20, 2.04
   Ⓒ 2.21, 2.20, 2.4, 2.04
   Ⓓ 2.20, 2.4, 2.04, 2.21

8. Which of the following numbers completes the sequence below?
   4.17, _____, 4.19

   Ⓐ 4.18
   Ⓑ 4.81
   Ⓒ 5.17
   Ⓓ 4.27

9. Which of the following comparisons is true?

   Ⓐ 0.403 > 0.304
   Ⓑ 0.043 < 0.403
   Ⓒ 0.043 < 0.304
   Ⓓ All of the above

10. Which number completes the following sequence?
    2.038, 2.039, _____

    Ⓐ 2.049
    Ⓑ 2.400
    Ⓒ 2.0391
    Ⓓ 2.04

11. Which of the following decimals is greater than 0.424 but less than 0.43.
    Circle the correct answer choice

    Ⓐ 0.4
    Ⓑ 0.423
    Ⓒ 0.431
    Ⓓ 0.429

12. **Order the following numbers from least to greatest.**
    1.003, 0.853, 0.85, 1.03, 0.96, 0.921
    Enter your answers in the correct order in the boxes given below

Chapter 3

Lesson 5: Rounding Decimals

You can scan the QR code given below or use the url to access additional EdSearch resources including videos and mobile apps related to *Rounding Decimals*.

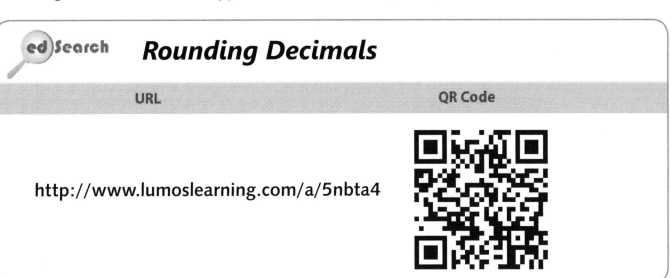

ed)Search   ***Rounding Decimals***

URL	QR Code
http://www.lumoslearning.com/a/5nbta4	

1. **Is $7.48 closest to $6, $7 or $8?**

   Ⓐ $6
   Ⓑ $7
   Ⓒ $8
   Ⓓ It is right in the middle of $7 and $8

2. **Round the Olympic time of 56.389 seconds to the nearest tenth of a second.**

   Ⓐ 56.0
   Ⓑ 57
   Ⓒ 56.4
   Ⓓ 56.39

3. **Round the number 57.81492 to the nearest hundredth.**

   Ⓐ 57.82
   Ⓑ 58.00
   Ⓒ 57.80
   Ⓓ 57.81

4. **Which of the following numbers would round to 13.75?**

   Ⓐ 13.755
   Ⓑ 13.70
   Ⓒ 13.756
   Ⓓ 13.747

5. **Jerry spent $5.91, $7.27, and $12.60 on breakfast, lunch, and dinner. Approximately how much did his meals cost in all?**

   Ⓐ about $24
   Ⓑ about $26
   Ⓒ about $25
   Ⓓ about $27

6. **Maria needs to buy wood for a door frame. She needs two pieces that are 6.21 feet long and one piece that is 2.5 feet long. About how much wood should she buy?**

   Ⓐ about 15 feet
   Ⓑ about 9 feet
   Ⓒ about 17 feet
   Ⓓ about 14 feet

7. Mika has a rectangular flower garden. It measures 12.2 meters on one side and 7.8 meters on the other. What is a reasonable estimation of the area of the flower garden? (Area= length x width)

Ⓐ 96 square meters
Ⓑ 20 square meters
Ⓒ 66 square meters
Ⓓ 120 square meters

8. Shanda ran a lap in 6.78 minutes. Assuming she maintains this time for every lap she runs, estimate the time it would take her to run three laps.

Ⓐ 25 minutes
Ⓑ 21 minutes
Ⓒ 18 minutes
Ⓓ 10 minutes

9. A basketball player scores an average of 13.2 points per game. During a 62-game season, he would be expected to score about _____ points. (Assume he will play every game.)

Ⓐ 600 points
Ⓑ 1,000 points
Ⓒ 800 points
Ⓓ 400 points

10. Use estimation to complete the following:
The difference of 31.245 - 1.396 is between _____.

Ⓐ 29 and 29.5
Ⓑ 29.5 and 30
Ⓒ 30 and 30.5
Ⓓ 30.5 and 31

11. When rounding to the nearest one's place, which of the following results in 430? More than one option may be correct. Select all the correct answers.

Ⓐ 429.67
Ⓑ 430.49
Ⓒ 429.365
Ⓓ 430.05

12. Read each statement below and mark the correct column to indicate whether you must round up or keep the digit.

	Round Up	Keep
Round 5.483 to the nearest hundredth.	○	○
Round 6.625 to the nearest tenth.	○	○
Round 77.951 to the nearest one.	○	○
Round 172.648 to the nearest hundredth.	○	○

13. Which of the following is rounded incorrectly?
    Circle the correct answer choice.

Ⓐ 226.35 to the nearest tenth is 226.4.
Ⓑ 1,430.49 to the nearest one is 1,431.
Ⓒ 0.318 to the nearest tenth is 0.3.
Ⓓ 10.067 to the nearest hundredth is 10.07

Chapter 3

You can scan the QR code given below or use the url to access additional EdSearch resources including videos and mobile apps related to *Multiplication of Whole Numbers*.

 Search | ***Multiplication of Whole Numbers***

URL	QR Code
http://www.lumoslearning.com/a/5nbtb5	

1. Solve. 79 x 14 = _____

   Ⓐ 790
   Ⓑ 1,106
   Ⓒ 854
   Ⓓ 224

2. A farmer plants 18 rows of beans. If there are 50 bean plants in each row, how many plants will he have altogether?

   Ⓐ 908
   Ⓑ 68
   Ⓒ 900
   Ⓓ 98

3. Solve. 680 x 94 = _____

   Ⓐ 64,070
   Ⓑ 63,960
   Ⓒ 64,760
   Ⓓ 63,920

4. What is the missing value?
   _____ x 11 = 374

   Ⓐ 36
   Ⓑ 30
   Ⓒ 34
   Ⓓ 31

5. Which of the following statements is true?

   Ⓐ 28 x 17 = 17 x 28
   Ⓑ 28 x 17 = 20 x 8 x 10 x 7
   Ⓒ 28 x 17 = (28 x 1) + (28 x 7)
   Ⓓ 28 x 17 = 27 x 18

6. **Which equation is represented by this array?**

Ⓐ 3 + 7 + 3 + 7 = 20
Ⓑ 7 + 7 + 7 + 7 + 7 = 35
Ⓒ 3 x 3 + 7 = 16
Ⓓ 3 x 7 = 21

7. **What would be a quick way to solve 596 x 101 accurately?**

Ⓐ Multiply 5 x 101, 9 x 101, 6 x 101, then add the products.
Ⓑ Multiply 596 x 100 then add 596 more.
Ⓒ Shift the 1 and multiply 597 x 100 instead.
Ⓓ Estimate 600 x 100.

8. **Harold baked 9 trays of cookies for a party. Three of the trays held 15 cookies each and six of the trays held 18 cookies each. How many cookies did Harold bake in all?**

Ⓐ 297
Ⓑ 135
Ⓒ 153
Ⓓ 162

9. **What's wrong with the following computation?**

```
      2 8
    x 5 3
    -------
      3 2
      6 0
    4 0 0
  + 1 0 0 0
    -------
    1 4 9 2
```

Ⓐ 3 x 8 is multiplied incorrectly.
Ⓑ 50 x 20 should only have two zeros.
Ⓒ 5 x 8 is only 40.
Ⓓ There's a missing 1 that should have been carried from the tens to the hundreds place.

10. Solve.
    407 x 35 = _____

    Ⓐ 14,280
    Ⓑ 14,245
    Ⓒ 12,445
    Ⓓ 16,135

11. Find the product.
    673 x 14 = _____

12. What is the product of 1620 x 944.
    Circle the correct answer choice.

    Ⓐ 27,540
    Ⓑ 1,529,280
    Ⓒ 217,080
    Ⓓ 942,180

13. Callie is calculating the product of 268 x 5,321. Help her complete the table below.

268	×	1	=	268
268	×		=	5,360
	×	300	=	80,400
268	×		=	
	×	Total	=	

14. What is the product of 321 X 1854
    Enter your answer in the box given below.

Chapter 3

Lesson 7: Division of Whole Numbers

You can scan the QR code given below or use the url to access additional EdSearch resources including videos and mobile apps related to *Division of Whole Numbers*.

 Division of Whole Numbers

URL	QR Code
http://www.lumoslearning.com/a/5nbtb6	

1. Find the missing number:
   48 ÷ ___ = 12

   Ⓐ 4
   Ⓑ 10
   Ⓒ 6
   Ⓓ 8

2. Hannah is filling gift bags for a party. She has 72 pieces of candy to pass out. If there are 8 bags, how many pieces of candy will go in each bag?

   Ⓐ 8
   Ⓑ 10
   Ⓒ 9
   Ⓓ 7

3. Solve. 1,248 ÷ 6 =

   Ⓐ 2,080
   Ⓑ 208
   Ⓒ 28
   Ⓓ 280

4. The fifth grade class took a field trip to the theater. The 96 students sat in rows with 10 students in each row. How many rows did they use?

   Ⓐ 11
   Ⓑ 9
   Ⓒ 10
   Ⓓ 12

5. What is the value of 6,720 ÷ 15?

   Ⓐ 510
   Ⓑ 426
   Ⓒ 448
   Ⓓ 528

6 What is 675,000 divided by 100?

   Ⓐ 675
   Ⓑ 67,500
   Ⓒ 67.5
   Ⓓ 6,750

7. **Which of the following statements is true?**

   Ⓐ $75 \div 0 = 0$
   Ⓑ $75 \div 0 = 1$
   Ⓒ $75 \div 0 = 75$
   Ⓓ $75 \div 0$ cannot be solved

8. **Taylor is putting 100 donuts into boxes. Each box holds 12 donuts. How many donuts will be left over after filling the last box fully?**

   Ⓐ 4
   Ⓑ 8
   Ⓒ 9
   Ⓓ 5

9. **Which of the following statements is true?**

   Ⓐ $26 \div 1 = 1$
   Ⓑ $26 \div 1 = 26$
   Ⓒ $26 \div 1 = 0$
   Ⓓ $26 \div 1$ cannot be solved

10. **Jeremy is rolling coins to take to the bank. He has 680 nickels to roll. If each sleeve holds 40 nickels, how many sleeves will he be able to fill?**

    Ⓐ 8
    Ⓑ 17
    Ⓒ 16
    Ⓓ 12

11. **Which of the following equations is true? Select the two correct answers.**

    Ⓐ $432 \div 12 = 36$
    Ⓑ $432 \div 8 = 44$
    Ⓒ $432 \div 18 = 24$
    Ⓓ $432 \div 16 = 30$

12. Read the following math sentences and indicate which are true and which are false.

	True	False
385 ÷ 35 > 12	○	○
1,680 ÷ 48 = 35	○	○
4,088 ÷ 56 = 75	○	○
884 ÷ 26 < 36	○	○

13. Which of the following completes the equation 564 ÷ _____ = 47
Circle the correct answer choice

Ⓐ 13
Ⓑ 18
Ⓒ 12
Ⓓ 28

14. Divide 388 by 15.
Enter the answer in the box given below

15. 6,720 ÷ 15 = _____

Chapter 3

Lesson 8: Add, Subtract, Multiply, & Divide Decimals

You can scan the QR code given below or use the url to access additional EdSearch resources including videos and mobile apps related to *Add, Subtract, Multiply, & Divide Decimals*.

ed)Search ***Add, Subtract, Multiply, & Divide Decimals***

URL	QR Code
http://www.lumoslearning.com/a/5nbtb7	

1. At a math competition, three members of a team each solved a problem as quickly as they could. Their times were 4.18 seconds, 3.75 seconds, and 3.99 seconds. What was the total of their times?

   Ⓐ 11.92 seconds
   Ⓑ 10.99 seconds
   Ⓒ 10.72 seconds
   Ⓓ 11.72 seconds

2. Beginning with the number 6.472, add:
   1 hundredth
   3 ones
   5 tenths
   What is the result?

   Ⓐ 7.822
   Ⓑ 6.823
   Ⓒ 9.982
   Ⓓ 6.607

3. Find the perimeter (total length of all four sides) of a trapezoid whose sides measure 2.09 ft, 2.09 ft, 3.72 ft, and 6.60 ft.

   Ⓐ 16.12 ft
   Ⓑ 14.5 ft
   Ⓒ 13.50 ft
   Ⓓ 8.56 ft

4. Find the difference:
   85.37 - 75.2 =

   Ⓐ 160.57
   Ⓑ 10
   Ⓒ 10.35
   Ⓓ 10.17

5. Subtract:
   3.64 - 1.46 =

   Ⓐ 2.18
   Ⓑ 4.18
   Ⓒ 1.18
   Ⓓ 4.20

6. Normal body temperature is 98.6 degrees Fahrenheit. When Tyler had a fever, his temperature went up to 102.2 degrees. By how much did Tyler's temperature increase?

Ⓐ 4.4 degrees
Ⓑ 3.6 degrees
Ⓒ 4.2 degrees
Ⓓ 3.2 degrees

7. A stamp costs $0.42. How much money would you need to buy 8 stamps?

Ⓐ $.82
Ⓑ $3.33
Ⓒ $3.36
Ⓓ $4.52

8. Find the product:
0.25 x 1.1 =

Ⓐ .75
Ⓑ 0.275
Ⓒ 0.27
Ⓓ .25

9. Divide 0.42 by 3.

Ⓐ 14
Ⓑ 126
Ⓒ 0.14
Ⓓ 12.6

10. Solve:
0.09 ÷ 0.3 =

Ⓐ 0.27
Ⓑ 0.003
Ⓒ 0.027
Ⓓ 0.3

11. Circle the number that is 5.47 more than 12.83 + 45.7

Ⓐ 68.53
Ⓑ 62.137
Ⓒ 64
Ⓓ 57.9

12. Solve:
    12.3 - 1.99 = _____

13. What decimal completes the equation in the table?
    Complete the table

3.5	×	4.01	=	

14. Solve:
    0.05 ÷ 0.2
    Enter your answer in the box below.

End of Numbers and Operations in Base Ten

Chapter 3:

Numbers and Operations in Base Ten

Answer Key
&
Detailed Explanations

Lesson 1: Place Value

Question No.	Answer	Detailed Explanations
1	B	The ten thousands place is five places to the left of the decimal, so the 1 is in the ten thousands place.
2	D	The thousandths place is three places to the right of the decimal, so the 6 is in the thousandths place.
3	A	The tenths place is immediately to the right of the decimal. In order to show eight-tenths, use an 8 immediately to the right of the decimal. It is common to use a place-holder 0 in the ones place.
4	C	Write the number 4 in the ones place. The word 'and' indicates the decimal point. The fractional part of the number is three-hundredths, which is shown with a 3 in the hundredths place. Use a placeholder 0 in the tenths place, so the 3 is two places to the right of the decimal.
5	A	The 6 is seven places to the left of the decimal, which is the millions place. Its value is 6 million.
6	C	The 9 is three places to the right of the decimal, which is the thousandths place. Its value is 9 thousandths.
7	D	In order for two numbers to be equal, they must have the same digits in the same place value. In this option, each number has a 5 in the tenths place. The following zeros after the tenths place do not change the value.
8	B	The hundredths place is two places to the right of the decimal. There is a 1 in the hundredths place, so one hundredth less would be 0, making the number 406.50.
9	A	The number 8.4 can be thought of as 8.40 (the final zero does not change the value). In this case, the number 8.41 would be greater because there is 1 hundredth compared to 0 hundredths. The other options are incorrect because they are equal to or less than 8.4 because the digit in the tenths place is lower.
10	D	21.7 has 2 in tens place and 2.17 has no digit in tens place. Therefore, 21.7 > 2.17. So, option (A) is incorrect. Number in option (B) has a greater digit (7) in the tenths place (2.17 has 1 in tenths place). Option (C) is equal to 2.17. The only option with a smaller digit in the tenths place is 2.07.

Question No.	Answer	Detailed Explanations
11	A & D	A digit in one place represents ten times more than the digit to its right and ten times less than the digit to its left. A. The digit 3 in 385.24 is three places to the right of the digit three in 452.38 and is thus 10 x 10 x 10 = 1000 times greater. Statement A is correct. B. The digit 5 in 452.38 is one place to the right of the digit 5 in 385.24 and is thus 10 times greater. Statement B is incorrect. C. The digit 8 in 385.24 is three places to the left of the digit 8 in 452.38 and is thus 10 x 10 x 10 = 1000 times greater. Statement C is incorrect. D. The digit 2 in 452.38 is one place to the left of the digit 2 in 385.24 and is thus 10 times greater. Statement D is correct.

12			Yes	No
		The 5 in 570.22 is ten times greater than 5 in 456.1.	●	○
		The 8 in 2.083 is hundred times less than the 8 in 328.7.	●	○
		The 3 in 1.039 is hundred times less than the 3 in 67.3.	○	●
		The 2 in 9,523 is thousand times more than the 2 in 45.92	●	○

The 5 in 570.22 is in the hundreds place. The 5 in 456.1 is in the tens place. Thus the 5 in 570.22 is ten times greater than the 5 in 456.1. Statement A is correct.

The 8 in 2.083 is in the hundredths place. The 8 in 328.7 is in the ones place. Thus the 8 in 2.083 is hundred times less than the 8 in 328.7. Statement B is correct.

The 3 in 1.039 is in the hundredths place. The 3 in 67.3 is in the tenths place. Thus the 3 in 1.039 is ten times less than the 3 in 67.3. Statement C is incorrect.

The 2 in 9,523 is in the tens place. The 2 in 45.92 is in the hundredths place. Thus the 2 in 9,523 is thousand times more than the 2 in 45.92. Statement D is correct.

Question No.	Answer	Detailed Explanations
13	Hundredths	The first digit to the right of a decimal point is the tenths place. The next digit to the right is the hundredths place. The correct answer is hundredths because the 3 is two places to the right of the decimal
14	A	The 7 in 539.7 is in the tenths place. A hundred times the tenths place is two places to the left or the tens place. The only answer choice with 7 in the tens place is 172.43. The correct answer is choice A.

Lesson 2: Multiplication & Division of Powers of Ten

Question No.	Answer	Detailed Explanations
1	B	10^3 means 10 x 10 x 10, which equals 1,000. 9 x 1,000 = 9,000. Another way to think of this problem is 9 x 10 = 90, then make sure the number of zeros in the answer matches the number of the exponent (3), which is 9,000.
2	B	10^7 means 10 x 10 x 10 x 10 x 10 x 10 x 10, which equals 10,000,000. Divide 10,000,000 by 100, or move the decimal point to the left (because it is division) two places to get 100,000.
3	A	Since the decimal point in 0.51 is being moved four places to the right, it is being multiplied by 10,000. This number can be shown as 10^4.
4	D	10^5 means 10 x 10 x 10 x 10 x 10, which equals 100,000. 3 x 100,000 = 300,000. Another way to think of this problem is 3 x 10 = 30, then make sure the number of zeros in the answer matches the number of the exponent (5), which is 300,000.
5	C	10^4 means 10 x 10 x 10 x 10, which equals 10,000. 6.9 ÷ 10,000 = 0.00069. Another way to think of this problem is to move the decimal in 6.9 to the left (because it is division) the number of places equal to the exponent (4).
6	B	The decimal point is being moved to the left, so it is a division problem. Since it is being moved 7 places, 8.2 is being divided by 10^7.
7	B	10^5 means 10 x 10 x 10 x 10 x 10, which equals 100,000. To find the number that is 100,000 times greater than 0.016, multiply 0.016 x 100,000, or move the decimal point to the right (because it is multiplication) the same number of places as the exponent (5).
8	C	Since the decimal point in 477.0 is being moved five places to the right, it is being multiplied by 100,000. This number can be shown as 10^5.
9	B	Since the decimal point in 113.0 is being moved three places to the left, it is being divided by 1,000. This number can be shown as 10^3.
10	D	10^5 means 10 x 10 x 10 x 10 x 10, which equals 100,000. Dividing by 100,000 is the same as moving the decimal place in five places to the left. Moving the decimal point in 4.6 five places back to the right would give you 460,000.

Question No.	Answer	Detailed Explanations

| 11 | | |

1,000,000	10^6
10,000	10^4
100	**10^2**
10,000,000	10^7

To write a multiple of ten as a power of ten, count the number of zeros. Then express the quantity as ten to the power of the number of zeros.
1,000,000 has six zeros, so as a power of ten, equals 10^6
10^4 represents $10 \times 10 \times 10 \times 10 = 10,000$.
100 has two zeros, so as a power of ten, equals 10^2
10^7 represents $10 \times 10 \times 10 \times 10 \times 10 \times 10 \times 10 = 10,000,000$.

| 12 | 10^3 | To write a multiple of ten as a power of ten, count the number of zeros. Then express the quantity as ten to the power of the number of zeros.
1,000 has three zeros so, as a power of ten, $1,000 = 10^3$ |
| 13 | B | To write a multiple of ten as a power of ten, count the number of zeros. Then express the quantity as ten to the power of the number of zeros.
100,000,000 has eight zeros so as a power of ten is 10^8. |

Lesson 3: Read and Write Decimals

Question No.	Answer	Detailed Explanations
1	A	The 4 goes in the hundredths place, which is two places to the right of the decimal. All other places get place-holder zeros.
2	C	The two is immediately to the right of the decimal, so it is in the tenths place. It is read "two tenths."
3	B	The fraction is seven tenths. To show this value in decimal form, use the digit 7 in the tenths place (immediately to the right of the decimal).
4	B	In the number 0.05, the 5 is in the hundredths place. To show this amount (five hundredths) as a fraction, use 5 as the numerator and 100 as the denominator.
5	D	One half is equal to five tenths (think of a pizza sliced into 10 pieces, half of the pizza would be 5 out of 10 slices). To show five tenths, use a 5 in the tenths place immediately to the right of the decimal.
6	A	Sixty hundredths is equivalent to six tenths (the place to the right of the decimal). Three hundredths is shown by a 3 in the hundredths place (two places to the right of the decimal).
7	C	Begin by saying the whole number (forty), the word 'and' for the decimal, and then the decimal portion of the number. The decimal .057 is fifty-seven thousandths. The 5 hundredths is equivalent to fifty thousandths.
8	C	The hundredths place (0) is two places to the right of the decimal. The tenths place (8) is immediately to the right of the decimal. The thousandths place (3) is three places to the right of the decimal. The ones place (9) is immediately to the left of the decimal.
9	D	In expanded form, each digit is multiplied by its place value and the products are added together. The expression $9 \times 10 + 2 \times 1 + 3 \times (\frac{1}{10}) + 8 \times (\frac{1}{100})$ can be thought of as: $9 \times 10 = 90$ $2 \times 1 = 2$ $3 \times (\frac{1}{10}) = .3$ $8 \times (\frac{1}{100}) = .08$ Add the products to get 92.38
10	B	In expanded form, each digit is multiplied by its place value and the products are added together. The number 0.85 is made up of 8 tenths, which is written as $8 \times (\frac{1}{10})$, and 5 hundredths, which is written as $5 \times (\frac{1}{100})$.

Question No.	Answer	Detailed Explanations
11	B & D	A. The first three digits of 452.25 have been expanded properly. The last two digits of 452.25 represent a value less than one. The two is in the tenths places and the 5 is in the hundreds place. Written in expanded form this is $2 \times (\frac{1}{10}) + 5 \times (\frac{1}{100})$ Thus $4 \times 100 + 5 \times 10 + 2 \times 1 + 2 \times 1 + 5 \times 10$ is an incorrect expansion.

A. The first three digits of 452.25 have been expanded properly. The last two digits of 452.25 represent a value less than one. The two is in the tenths places and the 5 is in the hundreds place. Written in expanded form this is $2 \times (\frac{1}{10}) + 5 \times (\frac{1}{100})$ Thus $4 \times 100 + 5 \times 10 + 2 \times 1 + 2 \times 1 + 5 \times 10$ is an incorrect expansion.

B. 53.81 has been expanded properly. $53.81 = 5 \times 10 + 3 \times 1 + 8 \times (\frac{1}{10}) + 1 \times (\frac{1}{100})$ is a correct expansion.

C. The first digit of 3.72 has been expanded properly. The digit 7 is in the tenths place and is expanded as $7 \times (1/10)$ and the digit two is in the hundredths place and expanded as $2 \times (1/100)$. Notice that the fraction have been flipped in answer choice C. $3.72 = 3 \times 1 + 7 \times (\frac{10}{1}) + 2 \times (\frac{100}{1})$ is an incorrect expansion.

D. 923.04 has been expanded properly. The nine is in the hundreds place, the 2 in the tens place, the 3 in the ones place and the 4 in the hundredths place. Notice that the zero in the tenths place is not included in the expansion. $9 \times 100 + 2 \times 10 + 3 \times 1 + 4 \times (\frac{1}{100})$ is a correct expansion.

The correct answer choices are B and D.

12			True	False
	345.3 = three hundred forty-five and three hundredths.		○	●
	$900 \times 30 \times 2 \times 4 \times (\frac{1}{10}) \times 7(\frac{1}{100}) >$ Nine hundred thirty-two and four hundredths		●	○
	$604.2 = 600 \times 4 \times 2 \times (\frac{1}{100})$		○	●
	1.805 > One and ninety-two hundredths		○	●

Rewrite each expanded form and number names as a number and compare.

$345.3 = 345.03 \rightarrow$ So, 1st statement is False

$900 \times 30 \times 2 \times 4 \times (\frac{1}{10}) \times 7 \times (\frac{1}{100}) = \frac{1512000}{1000} = 1512$ is greater than 932.04. So, 2nd statement is True.

$600 \times 4 \times 2 \times (\frac{1}{100}) = \frac{4800}{100} = 48$ is not equal to 604.2. So 3rd statement is False.

One and ninety-two hundredths = 1.92 is greater than 1.805. So, 4th statement is False.

Question No.	Answer	Detailed Explanations
13	79,417,608	The millions (79) are separated from the thousands (417) by a comma. Another comma separates the thousands from the hundreds (608). The first option has the correct place values but contains a number reversal on seventeen thousand.
14	C	Explanation A. Answer choice A does not have a four in the thousands place. Incorrect. B. Answer choice B has a four in the thousands place but the six is in the hundreds place. In addition the 13 is in the thousandths place. Incorrect. C. Answer choice C is correct. The four is in the thousands place, the six is in the tens place, the two is in the ones place and the 13 ends in the hundredths place. Correct. D. Answer choice D has a four in the thousands place but the six is in the hundreds place. Incorrect. The correct answer choice is C

Lesson 4: Comparing & Ordering Decimals

Question No.	Answer	Detailed Explanations
1	A	Since each of the options contains only one non-zero digit (4), compare the place value of the 4 to find the lowest number. 0.04 is the lowest number because the 4 is the furthest to the right of the decimal (in the hundredths place).
2	C	In order to find the greatest number, compare the digit in the highest place value. All of the options have 0 ones, so look to the tenths place. The number with 5 in the tenths place is greater than the numbers with 1 or 2 in the tenths place, no matter what comes next.
3	C	Seven hundredths is written 0.07. In order for a number to be lower, it has to have 0 in the tenths place and a digit lower than 7 in the hundredths place.
4	D	Each of these options involves comparing decimals (since the numbers to the left of the decimal point in each option are equal). Remember, the further a number is to the right of a decimal, the lower its place value. Be sure to compare numbers that are in the same place value (compare tenths to tenths, etc.). For each of these options, compare the underlined digit: 48.01 = 48.1 These are not equal, because .0 is less than .1. 25.4 < 25.40 The final zero does not affect the number's value, so these two numbers are equal. 10.83 < 10.093 The 8 in the tenths place is greater than a 0 in the tenths place. 392.01 < 392.1 This is correct because .1 is greater than .0.
5	C	In order to compare the size of numbers, begin with the place value furthest to the left. In this case, three of the numbers have a 1 in the ones place, so look to the tenths place to compare those three. The number with the lowest digit in the tenths place will come first (1.02) followed by the number with the next-highest digit in the tenths place (1.12) followed by the number with the highest digit in the tenths place (1.2). The remaining number has a 2 in the ones place, so it is the greatest.

Question No.	Answer	Detailed Explanations
6	C	Each of these options involves comparing similar digits in different place values. Be sure to compare numbers that are in the same place value (compare tenths to tenths, etc.), starting with the highest place value. For each of these options, compare the underlined digit: _3.21 > _32.1 No tens is less than 3 tens. _32.12 > _312.12 No hundreds is less than 3 hundreds. 32.12 > 3.212 This is correct because 3 tens is more than no tens. 212.3 < 21.32 Two hundreds is greater than no hundreds.
7	B	In order to compare the size of numbers, begin with the place value furthest to the left. In this case, all of the numbers have a 2 in the ones place, so look to the tenths place to compare them. The number with the highest digit in the tenths place will come first (2.4). The next two highest numbers both have a 2 in the tenths place, so look to the hundredths place. The number with the highest digit in the hundredths place will come first (2.21) followed by the number with the lower digit in the hundredths place (2.20). The final number has a 0 in the tenths place, so it is the least of all.
8	A	The missing number must be greater than 4.17 but less than 4.19. Since the ones place (4) and tenths place (1) are the same, the missing number will begin with 4.1 as well. Looking to the hundredths place, the missing number must fall between 7 and 9. That makes it 4.18.
9	D	To compare these numbers, look at the digit in the highest place value (the tenths place). 0.403 is greater than 0.304 and 0.043, as it has 4 in tenths place and the other two numbers have 3 and 0 in the tenths place respectively. Therefore options (A) and (B) are correct. In Option (C), we are comparing 0.043 with 0.304. 0.304 has 3 in tenths place and 0.043 has 0 in tenths place. Since 0 < 3, 0.043 < 0.304. So, option (C) is also correct. So, option (D) is the correct answer.
10	D	This pattern is increasing by one thousandth every term. After 2.039, the thousandth place will increase by one. Since there is already a 9 in the thousandths place, it will become zero and the hundredths place will increase to 4. The number 2.040 can also be written 2.04.

Question No.	Answer	Detailed Explanations
11	D	When comparing decimals align the decimal places and add zeros to the end of any decimal so all numbers have the same number of decimal places. Then compare the numbers ignoring the decimal point. 0.424 = 0.424 0.43 = 0.430 0.4 = 0.400 0.423 = 0.423 0.431 = 0.431 0.429 = 0.429 Now that each number has three decimal places, order the numbers ignoring the decimals. 400, 423, 424, 429, 430, 431. The only number between 424 (0.424) and 430 (0.43) is 429. Thus the correct answer is 0.429.
12	0.85 0.853 0.921 0.96 1.003 1.03	When comparing decimals, if the numbers do not have the same number of decimal places, add zeros to the end of the number until all numbers have the same number of decimals. Then compare the numbers ignoring the decimal point. 1.003, 0.853, 0.850, 1.030, 0.960, 0.921 – Now all numbers have three decimal points. 1003, 853, 850, 1030, 960, 921 – Ignore the decimal points. 850, 853, 921, 960, 1003, 1030 – Ordered from least to greatest 0.85, 0.853, 0.921, 0.96, 1.003, 1.03 – Decimals ordered from least to greatest

Lesson 5: Rounding Decimals

Question No.	Answer	Detailed Explanations
1	B	In order to round to the nearest whole dollar, look to the tenths (dimes) place. In $7.48 there is a 4 in the tenths place, which means round down to $7.00.
2	C	In the number 56.389, there is a 3 in the tenths place. Look to the right to see that 8 means round up. The number becomes 56.4 with no hundredths or thousandths.
3	D	In the number 57.81492, there is a 1 in the hundredths place. To determine whether to round up to 2 or remain 1, look to the digit to the right. A 4 means that the number will round down to 57.81.
4	D	In order for a number to round to 13.75, it must be between 13.745 and 13.754. The number 13.747 has a 7 in the thousandths place that means it will round up to 13.75.
5	B	Round $5.91 up to $6. Round $7.27 down to $7. Round $12.60 up to $13. $6 + $7 + $13 = $26.
6	C	Round 6.21 up to 7 and 2.5 up to 3. She needs two 7 feet pieces (=14 feet) and one 3 feet piece. She will have to buy about 17 feet (14 + 3) of wood.
7	A	Round each measurement to the nearest whole number, then multiply. 12.2 rounds down to 12 (because of the 2 in the tenths place) and 7.8 rounds up to 8 (because of the 8 in the tenths place). 12 x 8 = 96.
8	B	Round 6.78 to the nearest whole number. Since there is a 7 in the tenths place, round up (to the whole number 7). 7 x 3 = 21.
9	C	The answer options indicate that this problem can be solved using estimation. Round 13.2 down to 13 and 62 down to 60. 13 x 60 = 780, which is closest to the option '800 points.'
10	B	Round each number to the tenths place. 31.245 rounds down to 31.2 and 1.396 rounds up to 1.4. Think of 31.2 - 1.4 as 31.2 - 1.2 (which equals 30) minus another 0.2. That will put the answer slightly less than 30, so it is between 29.5 and 30.

Question No.	Answer	Detailed Explanations
11	A,B & D	The correct answer choices are A, B and D. When rounding to the one's place, look at the tenths place. If the tenth's digit is 5 or more, round the one's place to the next digit and drop the decimal digits. If the tenth's place is less than 5, keep the one's digit and drop the decimal digits.

A. Since the tenth's digit is 6 the one's digit is rounded up and the decimal digits are dropped so that 429.67 becomes 430. This is a correct answer choice.

B. Since the tenth's digit is 4 the one's digit is kept and the decimal digits are dropped so that 430.29 becomes 430. This is a correct answer choice.

C. Since the tenth's digit is 3 the one's digit is kept and the decimal digits are dropped so that 429.365 becomes 429. This is an incorrect answer choice.

D. Since the tenth's digit is 0 the one's digit is kept and the decimal digits are dropped so that 430.05 becomes 430. This is a correct answer choice.

12

	Round Up	Keep
Round 5.483 to the nearest hundredth.	○	●
Round 6.625 to the nearest tenth.	○	●
Round 77.951 to the nearest one.	●	○
Round 172.648 to the nearest hundredth.	●	○

When rounding, look at the digit to the right of the place to be rounded. If the digit is 5 or more, round to the next digit and drop the digits to the right. If the digit is less than 5, keep the number and drop the digits to the right.

A. When rounding 5.483 to the nearest hundredth, look at the thousands digit. Since the thousandths digit is 3, keep the hundredths digit and drop the numbers to the right. 5.483 rounded to the nearest hundredth is 5.48. KEEP

B. When rounding 6.625 to the nearest tenth, look at the hundredths digit. Since the hundredths digit is 2, keep the tenths digit and drop the numbers to the right. 6.625 rounded to the nearest tenth is 6.6. KEEP

C. When rounding 77.951 to the nearest one, look at the tenths digit. Since the tenths digit is 9, round the ones digit up to 8 and drop the numbers to the right. 77.951 rounded to the nearest one is 78. ROUND UP

D. When rounding 172.648 to the nearest hundredth, look at the thousandths digit. Since the thousandths digit is 8, round the hundredths digit up to 5 and drop the numbers to the right. 172.648 rounded to the nearest hundredth is 172.65. ROUND UP

Question No.	Answer	Detailed Explanations
13	B	When rounding, look at the digit to the right of the place to be rounded. If the digit is 5 or more, round to the next digit and drop the digits to the right. If the digit is less than 5, keep the number and drop the digits to the right. A. When rounding 226.35 to the nearest tenth, look at the hundredths digit. Since the hundredths digit is 5, round the tenths digit up to 4 and drop the numbers to the right. 226.35 rounded to the nearest tenth is 226.4. CORRECT B. When rounding 1430.49 to the nearest one, look at the tenths digit. Since the tenths digit is 4, keep the ones digit and drop the numbers to the right. 1,430.49 rounded to the nearest one is 1,430. INCORRECT – Drag this answer to the box. C. When rounding 0.318 to the nearest tenth, look at the hundredths digit. Since the hundredths digit is 1, keep the tenths digit and drop the numbers to the right. 0.318 rounded to the nearest tenth is 0.3. CORRECT D. When rounding 10.067 to the nearest hundredth, look at the thousandths digit. Since the thousandths digit is 7, round the hundredths digit up to 7 and drop the numbers to the right. 10.067 rounded to the nearest hundredth is 10.07. CORRECT The correct answer choice is B.

Lesson 6: Multiplication of Whole Numbers

Question No.	Answer	Detailed Explanations
1	B	$$\begin{array}{r} 79 \\ \times\ 14 \\ \hline 36 \\ 280 \\ 90 \\ +\ 700 \\ \hline 1106 \end{array}$$
2	C	This is a multiplication problem, because it is an array of 18 rows with 50 objects in each row. $$\begin{array}{r} 50 \\ \times\ 18 \\ \hline 0 \\ 400 \\ 0 \\ +\ 500 \\ \hline 900 \end{array}$$
3	D	$$\begin{array}{r} 680 \\ \times\ 94 \\ \hline 0 \\ 320 \\ 2400 \\ 0 \\ 7200 \\ +\ 54000 \\ \hline 63,920 \end{array}$$
4	C	Multiplying by 11 can be thought of as x 10 and x 1 more. 34 x 10 = 340 and 34 x 1 = 34. Together they equal 374. Alternate Method : We have to find the number, which, when multiplied with 11 gives 374. Number = 374/11. Use standard long division algorithm to find the number. Number = 34.

Question No.	Answer	Detailed Explanations
5	A	The Commutative Property of Multiplication states that when two factors are multiplied together, the product is the same no matter the order of the factors.
6	D	The array shows three rows with seven objects in each row. There are 21 objects in all. The array is called a 3 by 7 array, which is shown as $3 \times 7 = 21$.
7	B	According to the Distributive Property of Multiplication, you can break one of the factors (101) into two parts (100 and 1) and multiply them both by the other factor. 596×100 and 596×1 will produce the same answer as multiplying 596×100 and adding 596 more.
8	C	Three of the trays held 15 cookies each, so $3 \times 15 = 45$. The other six trays held 18 cookies each, so $6 \times 18 = 108$. To find the total, add $45 + 108 = 153$.
9	A	In the first step, 3×8 is recorded as 32. It should be 24.
10	B	$$\begin{array}{r} 407 \\ \times\ 35 \\ \hline 35 \\ 0 \\ 2000 \\ 210 \\ 0 \\ +\ 12000 \\ \hline 14{,}245 \end{array}$$
11	9,422	$$\begin{array}{r} 673 \\ \times\ 14 \\ \hline 12 \\ 280 \\ 2400 \\ 30 \\ 700 \\ 6000 \\ \hline 9{,}422 \end{array}$$

Question No.	Answer	Detailed Explanations

12	B	1620
		× 944
		   6480 1620 x 4
		  64800 1620 x 40
		<u>1458000</u> 1620 x 900
		1,529,280
		
		Answer Choice B (1,529,280) is the correct option.

Question 13:

When multiplying multi-digit numbers, multiply one number by each of the place value in the second number and then add the results together. The number 5321 in expanded form is 5000 + 300 + 20 + 1. Therefore the completed table is as follows:

268	×	1	=	268
268	×	**20**	=	5,360
268	×	300	=	80,400
268	×	**5000**	=	**1340000**
	×	Total	=	**1426028**

Question No.	Answer	Detailed Explanations

14	595,134	321
		× 1854
		    1284 321 x 4
		  16050 321 x 50
		256800 321 x 800
		<u>321000</u> 321 × 1000
		595,134

Lesson 7: Division of Whole Numbers

Question No.	Answer	Detailed Explanations
1	A	The equation $48 \div \_\_\_ = 12$ can be thought of as $48 \div 12 = \_\_\_$. There are 4 twelves in 48. Check the work by using multiplication ($4 \times 12 = 48$).
2	C	To solve the problem, divide 72 by 8. 72 can be divided evenly by 8. Check the work by using multiplication ($8 \times 9 = 72$).
3	B	1248 divided by 6 is 208 with remainder 0 = 208 R 0 = $208\ \frac{0}{6}$ **Show Work:**
4	C	Divide the number of students by the number of seats in each row. $96 \div 10 = 9$ R 6. The remaining 6 students still had to sit in a row, even though it was not full. The answer is 10 rows.
5	C	6720 divided by 15 is 448 with remainder 0 = 448 R 0 = $448\ \frac{0}{15}$ **Show Work:**

Question 3 Show Work:

```
    0 2 0 8
6 | 1 2 4 8
    0
    1 2
    1 2
      0 4
        0
        4 8
        4 8
          0
```

Question 5 Show Work:

```
      0 4 4 8
15 | 6 7 2 0
      0
      6 7
      6 0
        7 2
        6 0
          1 2 0
          1 2 0
              0
```

Question No.	Answer	Detailed Explanations
6	D	To divide by 100, move the decimal point two places to the left. When a whole number ending with zeroes is the dividend, take off as many 0's as appear in the divisor from the dividend to get the quotient.
7	D	No number that can be divided by zero.
| 8 | A | 100 divided by 12<br>is 8 with remainder 4<br>= 8 R 4<br>= $8 \frac{4}{12}$<br><br>**Show Work:**<br><br>```
      0 0 8
1 2 | 1 0 0
      0
      1 0
        0
      1 0 0
        9 6
          4
```<br><br>After filling 8 boxes, there will be a remainder of 4 donuts. |
| 9 | B | Any number divided by 1 remains the same. |
| 10 | B | 680 divided by 40<br>is 17 with remainder 0<br>= 17 R 0<br>= $17 \frac{0}{14}$<br><br>**Show Work:**<br><br>```
      0 1 7
4 0 | 6 8 0
      0
      6 8
      4 0
      2 8 0
      2 8 0
          0
``` |

Question No.	Answer	Detailed Explanations
11	A and C	

A. 432÷12=36. CORRECT

```
    36
12)432
    36          12 x 3
     7
    72          bring down the 2
    72          12 x 6
     0
```

B. 432÷8=44. INCORRECT, 432÷8=54

```
    54
8)432
   40           8 x 5
    3
   32           bring down the 2
   32           8 x 4
    0
```

C. 432÷18=24. CORRECT

```
    24
18)432
    36          18 x 2
     7
    72          bring down the 2
    72          18 x 4
     0
```

D. 432÷16=30. INCORRECT, 432÷16=27

```
    27
16)432
    32          16 x 2
    11
   112          bring down the 2
   112          16 x 7
     0
```

The correct answer choices are A and C.

Question No.	Answer	Detailed Explanations

	True	False
385 ÷ 35 > 12	○	●
1,680 ÷ 48 = 35	●	○
4,088 ÷ 56 = 75	○	●
884 ÷ 26 < 36	●	○

12

A. 385÷35>12. False, 385÷35=11 and 11 < 12

```
   11
35)385
   35          35 x 1
    3
   35          bring down the 5
   35          35 x 1
    0
```

B. 1680÷48=35. TRUE

```
   35
48)1680
  144          48 x 3
   24
  240          bring down the 0
  240          48 x 5
    0
```

C. 4088÷56=75. FALSE, 4088÷56=73

```
   73
56)4088
  392          56 x 7
   16
  168          bring down the 8
  168          56 x 3
    0
```

D. 884÷26<36. TRUE, 884÷26=34 and 34<36

```
   34
26)884
   78          26 x 3
   10
  104          bring down the 2
  104          26 x 4
    0
```

Question No.	Answer	Detailed Explanations
13	C	To find the number that completes the equation, divide 564 by 47. $564 \div 47 = 12$ $\begin{array}{r} 12 \\ \hline 47)564 \end{array}$ $\quad \underline{47} \qquad\qquad 47 \times 1$ $\quad\;\; 9$ $\quad \underline{94} \qquad\qquad 47 \times 2$ $\quad\;\;\; 0$
14	25 R 13	Start by dividing the 300 by 15. If 15 x 2 = 30, then 15 x 20 = 300. There are 20 fifteens in 300. The 88 will not divide evenly by 15, but 75 will (15 x 5 = 75). That gives us 25 x 15 = 375. Use this total to determine the remainder (388 - 375 = 13). The answer is 25 R 13.
15	448	6720 divided by 15 is 448 with remainder 0 = 448 R 0 $= 448 \; \dfrac{0}{15}$ $\begin{array}{r} 0448 \\ \hline 15)6720 \\ \underline{0}\;\;\;\;\;\; \\ 67\;\;\; \\ \underline{60}\;\;\; \\ 72\;\; \\ \underline{60}\;\; \\ 120 \\ \underline{120} \\ 0 \end{array}$

Lesson 8: Add, Subtract, Multiply, & Divide Decimals

Question No.	Answer	Detailed Explanations
1	A	Add each number, maintaining the place value of the digits. Any time a sum exceeds 9, carry the tens to the next highest place value.

$$\begin{array}{r} 4.1\ 8 \\ 3.7\ 5 \\ +\ 3.9\ 9 \\ \hline 1\ 1.9\ 2 \\ \hline \end{array}$$

Question No.	Answer	Detailed Explanations
2	C	Add each number, maintaining the place value of the digits.

$$\begin{array}{r} 6.4\ 7\ 2 \\ 0.0\ 1 \\ 3 \\ +\ 0.5 \\ \hline 9.9\ 8\ 2 \\ \hline \end{array}$$

Question No.	Answer	Detailed Explanations
3	B	Add each number, maintaining the place value of the digits. Any time a sum exceeds 9, carry the tens to the next highest place value.

$$\begin{array}{r} 2.0\ 9 \\ 2.0\ 9 \\ 3.7\ 2 \\ +\ 6.6\ 0 \\ \hline 1\ 4.5\ 0 \\ \hline \end{array}$$

Question No.	Answer	Detailed Explanations
4	D	Subtract the numbers, keeping their place values in line. Bring the decimal straight down to the solution.

$$\begin{array}{r} 8\ 5.3\ 7 \\ -\ 7\ 5.2 \\ \hline 1\ 0.1\ 7 \\ \hline \end{array}$$

Question No.	Answer	Detailed Explanations
5	A	Subtract the numbers, keeping their place values in line. Bring the decimal straight down to the solution.

$$\begin{array}{r} \overset{5\ 14}{3.6\ 4} \\ -\ 1.4\ 6 \\ \hline 2.1\ 8 \end{array}$$

Question No.	Answer	Detailed Explanations
6	B	Subtract the numbers, keeping their place values in line. Bring the decimal straight down to the solution.

$$\begin{array}{r} \overset{0\ \ 9\ \ 11\ 12}{1\ 0\ 2.2} \\ -\ \ \ 9\ 8.6 \\ \hline 0\ 0\ 3.6 \end{array}$$

Question No.	Answer	Detailed Explanations
7	C	To solve, multiply without decimals. Then insert the decimal in your answer. Be sure the product has as many places to the right of the decimal as both factors.

$$\begin{array}{r} \$\ 0.4\ 2 \\ \times\ 8 \\ \hline 1\ 6 \\ +\ 3\ 2\ 0 \\ \hline \$\ 3.3\ 6 \end{array}$$

Question No.	Answer	Detailed Explanations
8	B	To solve, multiply without decimals. Then insert the decimal in your answer. Be sure the product has as many places to the right of the decimal as both factors.

$$\begin{array}{r} 0.2\ 5 \\ \times\ \ \ 1.1 \\ \hline 5 \\ 2\ 0 \\ 5\ 0 \\ 2\ 0\ 0 \\ \hline 0.2\ 7\ 5 \end{array}$$

Question No.	Answer	Detailed Explanations
9	C	To solve, use division. Divide the numbers without the decimal point. Then, insert a decimal into the answer, leaving the same number of places to the right of the decimal as the dividend. $42 \div 3 = 14 \rightarrow 0.14$
10	D	To solve, use division. Move both decimal places to the right one place, so you are dividing by a whole number ($0.9 \div 3$). Divide the numbers without the decimal point. Then, insert a decimal into the answer, leaving the same number of places to the right of the decimal as the dividend (remember that you shifted the decimal to have only one place to the right of the dividend). $9 \div 3 = 3 \rightarrow 0.3$
11	C	When adding decimals, line up the decimals and add any necessary zeros to the end of the numbers so they have the same number of decimal places. Then add each place value as normal bringing down the decimal in the same location as in the original numbers. 12.83 45.70 +5.47 64.00
12	10.31	Subtract the numbers, keeping their place values in line. Bring the decimal straight down to the solution. Remember that the number 12.3 can be written as 12.30. 1 12 10 12. 3̶ 0̶ - 1. 9 9 1 0. 3 1
13	14.035	<table><tr><td>3.5</td><td>×</td><td>4.01</td><td>=</td><td>14.035</td></tr></table>When multiplying decimals, multiply as normal ignoring the decimal point. Then count the number of decimal places in the factors. The answer should have the same number of decimal places as the factors combined. 35 × 401 35 000 14000 14035 There is one decimal place in 3.5 and two decimal places in 4.01 so the answer should have $1 + 2 = 3$ decimal places. Counting from the back of the answer, the decimal goes in front of the zero. The answer is 14.035

Question No.	Answer	Detailed Explanations
14	0.25	To solve, use division. Move both decimal places to the right one place, so you are dividing by a whole number (0.5 ÷ 2). Since 5 will not divide evenly by 2, think of it as 0.50. Divide the numbers without the decimal point. Then, insert a decimal into the answer, leaving the same number of places to the right of the decimal as the dividend (remember that you used 0.50, so there should be two places to the right of the decimal in your answer). 50 ÷ 2 = 25 →0.25

Chapter 4:
Number & Operations - Fractions

Lesson 1: Add & Subtract Fractions

You can scan the QR code given below or use the url to access additional EdSearch resources including videos and mobile apps related to *Add & Subtract Fractions*.

 **Add & Subtract Fractions**

URL	QR Code
http://www.lumoslearning.com/a/5nfa1	

1. Add: $\dfrac{2}{10} + \dfrac{1}{10} =$

   Ⓐ $\dfrac{3}{20}$

   Ⓑ $\dfrac{3}{10}$

   Ⓒ $\dfrac{1}{10}$

   Ⓓ $\dfrac{2}{10}$

2. To make a bowl of punch, Joe mixed $1\dfrac{1}{4}$ gallons of juice with $1\dfrac{2}{4}$ gallons of sparkling water. How much punch does he have?

   Ⓐ $2\dfrac{3}{4}$ gallons

   Ⓑ 3 gallons

   Ⓒ $\dfrac{1}{4}$ gallon

   Ⓓ $\dfrac{3}{4}$ gallon

3. Subtract: $\dfrac{3}{4} - \dfrac{2}{4} =$

   Ⓐ $\dfrac{5}{4}$

   Ⓑ $\dfrac{1}{4}$

   Ⓒ $\dfrac{3}{4}$

   Ⓓ 1

4. Subtract: $3\dfrac{4}{10} - 1\dfrac{1}{10} =$

   Ⓐ $1\dfrac{3}{10}$

   Ⓑ $2\dfrac{1}{10}$

   Ⓒ $3\dfrac{3}{10}$

   Ⓓ $2\dfrac{3}{10}$

5. To add the fractions $\frac{3}{4}$ and $\frac{7}{12}$, what must first be done?

    Ⓐ Reduce the fractions to lowest terms
    Ⓑ Change to improper fractions
    Ⓒ Make the numerators the same
    Ⓓ Find a common denominator

6. Add: $\frac{1}{2} + \frac{1}{4} =$

    Ⓐ $\frac{2}{6}$

    Ⓑ $\frac{2}{3}$

    Ⓒ $\frac{3}{4}$

    Ⓓ $\frac{1}{2}$

7. Find the difference: $\frac{2}{3} - \frac{1}{9} =$

    Ⓐ $\frac{1}{6}$

    Ⓑ $\frac{5}{9}$

    Ⓒ $\frac{3}{12}$

    Ⓓ $\frac{2}{27}$

8. Find the sum: $2\frac{1}{8} + 5\frac{1}{2} =$

    Ⓐ $7\frac{2}{10}$

    Ⓑ $10\frac{1}{16}$

    Ⓒ $3\frac{1}{6}$

    Ⓓ $7\frac{5}{8}$

9. Find the sum of five and five eighths plus one and one fourth.

  Ⓐ $6\dfrac{7}{8}$

  Ⓑ $10\dfrac{6}{8}$

  Ⓒ $6\dfrac{6}{12}$

  Ⓓ $7\dfrac{2}{10}$

10. Subtract: $5 - \dfrac{1}{3} =$

  Ⓐ $5\dfrac{1}{3}$

  Ⓑ $4\dfrac{1}{3}$

  Ⓒ $3\dfrac{2}{3}$

  Ⓓ $4\dfrac{2}{3}$

11. Jordan had a plank of wood that was $8\dfrac{5}{16}$ inches long. He sawed off $2\dfrac{3}{16}$ inches. Now how long is the plank of wood?

  Ⓐ $10\dfrac{8}{32}$ inches

  Ⓑ $6\dfrac{1}{4}$ inches

  Ⓒ $6\dfrac{2}{16}$ inches

  Ⓓ $10\dfrac{8}{16}$ inches

12. At the beginning of 5th grade, Amber's hair was $8\dfrac{1}{2}$ inches long. By the end of 5th grade it was $10\dfrac{3}{4}$ inches long. How many inches did Amber's hair grow during 5th grade?

  Ⓐ $19\dfrac{1}{4}$ inches

  Ⓑ $18\dfrac{4}{6}$ inches

  Ⓒ $2\dfrac{1}{2}$ inches

  Ⓓ $2\dfrac{1}{4}$ inches

13. Solve: $\dfrac{1}{5} + \dfrac{3}{5} + \dfrac{4}{5} =$ _____

14. Find the missing number: $4\dfrac{1}{4} +$ _____ $= 7\dfrac{1}{2}$

   Ⓐ $3\dfrac{1}{4}$

   Ⓑ $3\dfrac{3}{4}$

   Ⓒ $3\dfrac{1}{2}$

   Ⓓ $2\dfrac{3}{4}$

15. Solve: $\dfrac{7}{10} - \left(\dfrac{4}{10} - \dfrac{1}{10}\right) =$

   Ⓐ $\dfrac{2}{10}$

   Ⓑ $\dfrac{4}{10}$

   Ⓒ 0

   Ⓓ $\dfrac{3}{10}$

16. Which of the following expression(s) is equivalent to $\dfrac{2}{3} + \dfrac{7}{4}$?
Select all the correct answers

   Ⓐ $\dfrac{4}{6} + \dfrac{9}{6}$

   Ⓑ $\dfrac{8}{12} + \dfrac{21}{12}$

   Ⓒ $\dfrac{40}{60} + \dfrac{105}{60}$

   Ⓓ $\dfrac{12}{16} + \dfrac{28}{16}$

   Ⓒ $\dfrac{20}{36} + \dfrac{54}{36}$

17. What is the value of $\dfrac{3}{5} - \dfrac{2}{7}$

Write your answer in the box given below

Chapter 4

Lesson 2: Problem Solving with Fractions

You can scan the QR code given below or use the url to access additional EdSearch resources including videos and mobile apps related to *Problem Solving with Fractions*.

 **Problem Solving with Fractions**

URL	QR Code
http://www.lumoslearning.com/a/5nfa2	

1. Susan's homework was to practice the piano for $\frac{3}{4}$ of an hour each night. How many minutes each night did she practice?

   Ⓐ 30 minutes
   Ⓑ 15 minutes
   Ⓒ 45 minutes
   Ⓓ 60 minutes

2. Three fifths of the 30 students are boys. How many students are girls?

   Ⓐ 12 girls
   Ⓑ 18 girls
   Ⓒ 6 girls
   Ⓓ 8 girls

3. Walking at a steady pace, Ella walked 11 miles in 3 hours. Which mixed number shows how many miles she walked in an hour?

   Ⓐ $\frac{2}{3}$
   Ⓑ $2\frac{2}{3}$
   Ⓒ 3
   Ⓓ $3\frac{2}{3}$

4. In science class we discovered that $\frac{7}{8}$ of an apple is water. What fraction of the apple is not water?

   Ⓐ $\frac{1}{6}$
   Ⓑ $\frac{1}{7}$
   Ⓒ $\frac{7}{8}$
   Ⓓ $\frac{1}{8}$

5. There were 20 pumpkins in a garden. One fourth of the pumpkins were too small, one tenth were too large, and one half were just the right size. The rest were not ripe yet. How many of the pumpkins were too small?

   Ⓐ 3
   Ⓑ 2
   Ⓒ 5
   Ⓓ 10

6. Timothy decided to clean out his closet by donating some of his 45 button-down shirts. He gave away 9 shirts. What fraction of the shirts did he give away?

   Ⓐ $\frac{1}{5}$

   Ⓑ $\frac{1}{9}$

   Ⓒ $\frac{1}{2}$

   Ⓓ $\frac{36}{45}$

7. There are 32 students in Mr. Duffy's class. If 4 come to after school tutoring, what fraction of the class comes to after school tutoring?

   Ⓐ $\frac{28}{32}$

   Ⓑ $\frac{1}{8}$

   Ⓒ $\frac{1}{4}$

   Ⓓ $\frac{2}{8}$

8. Dara has to solve 35 math problems for homework. She has completed 14 of them. What fraction of the problems does she have left to do?

   Ⓐ $\frac{14}{35}$

   Ⓑ $\frac{3}{5}$

   Ⓒ $\frac{14}{21}$

   Ⓓ $\frac{2}{5}$

9. A 5th grade volleyball team scored 32 points in one game. Of those points, $\frac{2}{8}$ were scored in the second half. How many points were scored in the first half of the game?

   Ⓐ 12
   Ⓑ 4
   Ⓒ 20
   Ⓓ 24

10. A recipe to make 48 cookies calls for 3 cups of flour. However, you do not want to make 48 cookies, but only 24 cookies. Which fraction shows how much flour to use?

Ⓐ 2 cups

Ⓑ $1\frac{2}{3}$ cups

Ⓒ $1\frac{1}{2}$ cups

Ⓓ $2\frac{2}{3}$ cups

11. Match the statement with the symbol that will make the statement true

	>	<	=
$\frac{5}{6} - \frac{2}{3} \square \frac{1}{2} - \frac{3}{8}$	○	○	○
$\frac{5}{6} + \frac{2}{3} \square \frac{3}{4} + \frac{5}{12}$	○	○	○
$\frac{3}{15} + \frac{2}{5} \square \frac{1}{3} + \frac{2}{5}$	○	○	○
$\frac{7}{8} - \frac{1}{4} \square \frac{3}{4} - \frac{1}{8}$	○	○	○

12. A recipe calls for $\frac{1}{2}$ pound of butter. If there is $\frac{5}{8}$ of a pound, how much (pounds) of butter is left after the cooking? Circle the correct answer.

Ⓐ $\frac{1}{8}$

Ⓑ $\frac{5}{4}$

Ⓒ $\frac{2}{3}$

Ⓓ $\frac{5}{16}$

13. Forest bought a can of paint to paint his drone. If the first coat of paint used $\frac{2}{3}$ of the can of paint and the second coat used $\frac{2}{15}$ of the can, select the correct equation to determine the fraction of the paint used on the drone? Circle on the correct answer.

Ⓐ $\frac{2}{15} - \frac{2}{3} = \frac{2}{15} - \frac{10}{15} = -\frac{8}{15}$

Ⓑ $\frac{2}{3} + \frac{2}{5} = \frac{10}{15} + \frac{2}{15} = \frac{12}{15} = \frac{4}{5}$

Ⓒ $\frac{2}{3} - \frac{2}{15} = \frac{10}{15} - \frac{2}{15} = \frac{(10-2)}{15} = \frac{8}{15}$

Ⓓ $\frac{2}{3} \times \frac{2}{15} = \frac{4}{45}$

Chapter 4

Lesson 3: Interpreting Fractions

You can scan the QR code given below or use the url to access additional EdSearch resources including videos and mobile apps related to *Interpreting Fractions*.

 Interpreting Fractions

URL	QR Code
http://www.lumoslearning.com/a/5nfb3	

1. Suppose three friends wanted to share four cookies equally. How many cookies would each friend receive?

   Ⓐ $1\dfrac{1}{3}$

   Ⓑ $\dfrac{3}{4}$

   Ⓒ $1\dfrac{3}{4}$

   Ⓓ $\dfrac{1}{3}$

2. If 18 is divided by 5, which fraction represents the remainder divided by divisor?

   Ⓐ $\dfrac{3}{18}$

   Ⓑ $\dfrac{3}{5}$

   Ⓒ $\dfrac{5}{18}$

   Ⓓ $\dfrac{1}{3}$

3. If there are 90 minutes in a soccer game and 4 squads of players will share this time equally, how many minutes will each squad play?

   Ⓐ $\dfrac{22}{4}$

   Ⓑ $22\dfrac{1}{2}$

   Ⓒ $22\dfrac{2}{10}$

   Ⓓ $18\dfrac{4}{22}$

4. Damien has $695 in the bank. He wants to withdraw $\dfrac{2}{5}$th of his money. If he uses a calculator to figure out this amount, which buttons should he press?

   Ⓐ [6] [9] [5] [x] [2] [x] [5] [=]
   Ⓑ [6] [9] [5] [÷] [2] [x] [5] [=]
   Ⓒ [6] [9] [5] [÷] [2] [÷] [5] [=]
   Ⓓ [6] [9] [5] [x] [2] [÷] [5] [=]

5. Five friends are taking a trip in a car. They want to share the driving equally. If the trip takes 7 hours, how long should each friend drive?

Ⓐ $\frac{5}{7}$ of an hour

Ⓑ 1 hour 7 minutes

Ⓒ $1\frac{2}{5}$ hours

Ⓓ 1 hour 2 minutes

6. Which fraction is equivalent to 3 ÷ 10?

Ⓐ $\frac{1}{3}$

Ⓑ $\frac{10}{3}$

Ⓒ $\frac{13}{3}$

Ⓓ $\frac{3}{10}$

7. Which number completes this equation?
$$\frac{5}{8} = 5 \div \underline{\quad}$$

Ⓐ 13

Ⓑ $\frac{1}{5}$

Ⓒ 8

Ⓓ $\frac{1}{8}$

8. If 9 people want to share a birthday cake equally, what fraction of the cake will each person get?

Ⓐ $\frac{8}{9}$

Ⓑ $\frac{1}{9}$

Ⓒ $\frac{1}{2}$

Ⓓ $\frac{9}{2}$

9. Which number completes this equation?

$$\frac{4}{7} \times 7 = \underline{\quad}$$

Ⓐ 4

Ⓑ 28

Ⓒ $\frac{4}{49}$

Ⓓ $\frac{21}{7}$

10. Which number completes this equation?

$$\frac{2}{3} = \underline{\quad} \div 3$$

Ⓐ 3

Ⓑ $\frac{1}{2}$

Ⓒ 2

Ⓓ $\frac{1}{3}$

11. Sinclair made 6 points out of the team's total of 24 points. What fraction of the team's total points did Sinclair make? Select all the correct answers.

Ⓐ $\frac{2}{5}$

Ⓑ $\frac{6}{24}$

Ⓒ $\frac{1}{4}$

Ⓓ $\frac{2}{6}$

12. Justine found 6-feet of string with which to make 8 bracelets. If each bracelet was the same length, how long was each bracelet? Enter your answer in the box as a fraction in its simplest form.

Chapter 4

Lesson 4: Multiply Fractions

You can scan the **QR code** given below or use the url to access additional EdSearch resources including videos and mobile apps related to *Multiply Fractions*.

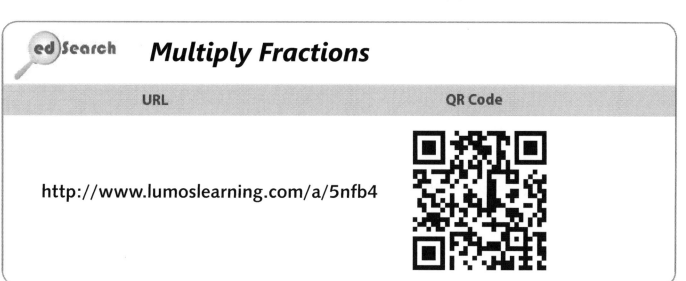

URL	QR Code
http://www.lumoslearning.com/a/5nfb4	

1. Multiply: $\dfrac{2}{3} \times \dfrac{4}{5} =$

   Ⓐ $\dfrac{8}{15}$

   Ⓑ $\dfrac{3}{4}$

   Ⓒ $\dfrac{6}{8}$

   Ⓓ $\dfrac{4}{15}$

2. Find the product: $5 \times \dfrac{2}{3} \times \dfrac{1}{2} =$

   Ⓐ $1\dfrac{1}{3}$

   Ⓑ 5

   Ⓒ $2\dfrac{2}{3}$

   Ⓓ $1\dfrac{2}{3}$

3. Which of the following is equivalent to $\dfrac{5}{6} \times 7$?

   Ⓐ $5 \div (6 \times 7)$
   Ⓑ $(5 \times 7) \div 6$
   Ⓒ $(6 \times 7) \div 5$
   Ⓓ $(1 \div 7) \times (5 \div 6)$

4. Which of the following is equivalent to $\dfrac{4}{10} \times \dfrac{3}{8}$?

   Ⓐ $4 \div (10 \times 3) \div 8$
   Ⓑ $(4 + 3) \times (10 + 8)$
   Ⓒ $(4 \times 3) \div (10 \times 8)$
   Ⓓ $(4 - 3) \div (10 - 8)$

5. Hector is using wood to build a dog house. Each wall is $\dfrac{4}{7}$ of a yard tall and $\dfrac{3}{5}$ of a yard wide. Knowing that the area of each wall is the base times the height, how many square yards of wood will he need to build 4 walls of equal size?

   Ⓐ $1\dfrac{2}{3}$

   Ⓑ $1\dfrac{13}{35}$

   Ⓒ $\dfrac{12}{35}$

   Ⓓ $1\dfrac{4}{12}$

6. An auditorium has 600 seats. One-third of the seats are empty. How many seats are empty?

Ⓐ 300 seats
Ⓑ 400 seats
Ⓒ 200 seats
Ⓓ 900 seats

7. Which of these numbers is not equivalent to the other three?

Ⓐ $\dfrac{44}{8}$

Ⓑ $5\dfrac{25}{50}$

Ⓒ $5\dfrac{1}{5}$

Ⓓ 5.500

8. Multiply: $\dfrac{1}{2} \times \dfrac{1}{4} =$

Ⓐ $\dfrac{1}{2}$

Ⓑ $\dfrac{1}{8}$

Ⓒ $\dfrac{2}{8}$

Ⓓ $2\dfrac{1}{2}$

9. What fraction is one half of three fourths?

Ⓐ $\dfrac{1}{3}$

Ⓑ $\dfrac{3}{4}$

Ⓒ $\dfrac{3}{8}$

Ⓓ $\dfrac{1}{8}$

10. One half of one tenth is what fraction?

Ⓐ $\dfrac{1}{5}$

Ⓑ $\dfrac{1}{20}$

Ⓒ $\dfrac{1}{10}$

Ⓓ $\dfrac{1}{2}$

11. Read each equation below and mark the box to indicate whether the equation is true or false.

	True	False
$4 \times \dfrac{3}{4} = 3$	○	○
$\dfrac{1}{6}$ of 7 is $\dfrac{6}{7}$	○	○
$\dfrac{1}{3} \times 9 = 3$	○	○
$10 \times \dfrac{1}{6} = 1\dfrac{2}{3}$	○	○

12. Fill in the table to complete the math sentence.

$\dfrac{1}{6}$	×		=	$\dfrac{3}{24}$	=	

13. Terry brought some chocolate for lunch and shared it evenly among himself and two friends. If his share was $\frac{1}{6}$ of a pound, how much chocolate did Terry bring to school? Circle the correct answer choice

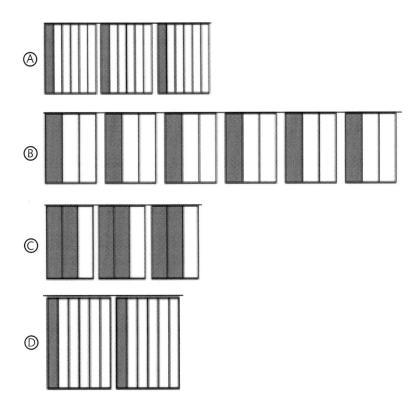

Chapter 4

Lesson 5: Multiply to Find Area

You can scan the QR code given below or use the url to access additional EdSearch resources including videos and mobile apps related to *Multiply to Find Area*.

Multiply to Find Area

URL	QR Code
http://www.lumoslearning.com/a/5nfb4b	

1. Dominique is covering the top of her desk with contact paper. The surface measures $\frac{7}{8}$ yard by $\frac{3}{4}$ yard. How much contact paper will she need to cover the surface of the desktop?

   Ⓐ $\frac{21}{32}$ yd²

   Ⓑ $\frac{13}{8}$ yd²

   Ⓒ $\frac{20}{24}$ yd²

   Ⓓ $1\frac{5}{8}$ yd²

2. Christopher is tiling his bathroom floor with tiles that are each 1 square foot. The floor measures $2\frac{1}{2}$ feet by $3\frac{3}{4}$ feet. How many tiles will he need to cover the floor?

   Ⓐ $6\frac{3}{8}$

   Ⓑ $6\frac{1}{4}$

   Ⓒ $9\frac{3}{8}$

   Ⓓ 8

3. Lin and Tyra are measuring the area of the piece of paper shown below. Lin multiplied the length times the width to find an answer. Tyra traced the paper onto 1-inch graph paper and counted the number of squares. How should their answers compare?

   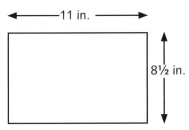

   Ⓐ Lin's answer will be a mixed number, but Tyra's will be a whole number.
   Ⓑ Tyra's answer will be greater than Lin's answer.
   Ⓒ Lin's answer will be greater than Tyra's answer.
   Ⓓ They should end up with almost exactly the same answer.

4. Jeremy found that it takes 14 centimeter cubes to cover the surface of a rectangular image. Which of these measurements could possibly be the length and width of the rectangle he covered? Assume that centimeter cubes can be cut so that fractional measurements are possible.

Ⓐ Length = $3\frac{1}{2}$ cm, width = 4 cm

Ⓑ Length = $4\frac{1}{2}$ cm, width = 3 cm

Ⓒ Length = 7 cm, width = 7 cm

Ⓓ Length = 7 cm, width = 3 cm

5. What is the area of the court shown below?

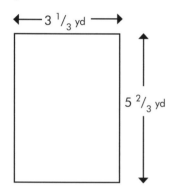

Ⓐ $15\frac{2}{9}$ yd²

Ⓑ $18\frac{8}{9}$ yd²

Ⓒ 16 yd²

Ⓓ 9 yd²

6. A rectangle has a width of $\frac{3}{5}$ and a length of $\frac{4}{9}$. Choose two of the following answers that correctly represent the area of the rectangle?

Ⓐ $\frac{47}{45}$

Ⓑ $\frac{12}{45}$

Ⓒ $\frac{1}{2}$

Ⓓ $\frac{4}{15}$

7. **Use the picture below to find the area of the rectangle. Enter your answer in the box.**

$\frac{5}{6}$ cm

2 cm

8. **Which of the following have an area less than one meter squared? Circle the correct answer choice.**

Ⓐ Length = $1\frac{3}{8}$ m; Width = $\frac{7}{9}$ sq m

Ⓑ Length = $2\frac{1}{6}$ m; Width = $\frac{3}{4}$ sq m

Ⓒ Length = $2\frac{5}{6}$ m; Width = $\frac{1}{3}$ sq m

Ⓓ Length = $1\frac{7}{8}$ m; Width = $\frac{4}{5}$ sq m

9. **Find the area of the rectangle**

$\frac{1}{2}$ m

$\frac{3}{4}$ m

10. **Evaluate $\frac{7}{12}$ x $\frac{1}{2}$**

Ⓐ $\frac{7}{24}$

Ⓑ $\frac{7}{6}$

Ⓒ $\frac{6}{7}$

Ⓓ $\frac{1}{7}$

Chapter 4

Lesson 6: Multiplication as Scaling

You can scan the QR code given below or use the url to access additional EdSearch resources including videos and mobile apps related to *Multiplication as Scaling*.

 Multiplication as Scaling

URL	QR Code
http://www.lumoslearning.com/a/5nfb5a	

1. If y is four times as much as z, which number completes this equation?
   z * ___ = y

   Ⓐ 4
   Ⓑ 0.4
   Ⓒ $\dfrac{1}{4}$
   Ⓓ 40

2. In the equation a * b = c, if b is a fraction greater than 1, then c will be _____.

   Ⓐ a mixed number
   Ⓑ less than b
   Ⓒ greater than a
   Ⓓ equal to b ÷ 10

3. If d * e = f, and e is a fraction less than 1, then f will be _____.

   Ⓐ greater than d
   Ⓑ less than d
   Ⓒ equal to e ÷ d
   Ⓓ less than 1

4. In which equation is r less than s?

   Ⓐ r - 6 = s
   Ⓑ s * 6 = r
   Ⓒ r ÷ 6 = s
   Ⓓ s * $\dfrac{1}{6}$ = r

5. Ryan and Alex are using beads to make necklaces. Ryan used one fifth as many beads as Alex. Which equation is true?
   (Take R = Number of beads used by Ryan, A = Number of beads used by Alex).

   Ⓐ R * $\dfrac{1}{5}$ = A
   Ⓑ R = A * 5
   Ⓒ R * 5 = A
   Ⓓ R ÷ 5 = A

6. **Which statement is true about this equation?**
   5 x t = u

   Ⓐ t divided by u equals 5
   Ⓑ t plus 5 equals u
   Ⓒ u times 5 equals t
   Ⓓ t is $\frac{1}{5}$th of u

7. **f is 100 times as much as g when:**

   Ⓐ g x 100 = f
   Ⓑ g + 100 = f
   Ⓒ f x 10 = g
   Ⓓ $\frac{1}{10}$ of f = g

8. **When multiplying 82 x 25, the product will be _____.**

   Ⓐ less than 10 times 82
   Ⓑ 100 times as much as 25
   Ⓒ 25 times as much as 82
   Ⓓ equal to 82 divided by 25

9. **In the equation 19 x 78 = m, which of the following is true?**

   Ⓐ m is 78 times as much as 19
   Ⓑ m is 19 times less than 78
   Ⓒ m is equal to 78 divided by 19
   Ⓓ m is 78 more than 19

10. **If j is three hundred times as much as k, which number completes this equation?**
    k x ___ = j

    Ⓐ $\frac{1}{30}$
    Ⓑ 300
    Ⓒ (3 + 100)
    Ⓓ 0.03

11. Read each comparison and indicate whether the comparison is true or false

	True	False
$\dfrac{7}{8} \times \dfrac{3}{4} > \dfrac{7}{8}$	◯	◯
$2\dfrac{1}{2} \times \dfrac{6}{5} < 2\dfrac{1}{2}$	◯	◯
$\dfrac{8}{15} \times \dfrac{1}{3} < \dfrac{1}{3}$	◯	◯
$\dfrac{11}{12} \times \dfrac{3}{2} < \dfrac{11}{12}$	◯	◯

12. Circle the fraction that will complete the statement below:

$3 \times ? > 3$

Ⓐ $\dfrac{2}{3}$

Ⓑ $\dfrac{7}{8}$

Ⓒ $\dfrac{6}{5}$

Ⓓ $\dfrac{3}{4}$

13. Enter <1 or >1 into the table below to complete a true comparison.

$\dfrac{8}{9}$	×	⬭	<	$\dfrac{8}{9}$
⬭	×	$1\dfrac{1}{5}$	<	$1\dfrac{1}{5}$
$\dfrac{5}{4}$	×	⬭	>	$\dfrac{5}{4}$

Chapter 4

Lesson 7: Numbers Multiplied by Fractions

You can scan the QR code given below or use the url to access additional EdSearch resources including videos and mobile apps related to *Numbers Multiplied by Fractions*.

 **Numbers Multiplied by Fractions**

URL	QR Code
http://www.lumoslearning.com/a/5nfb5b	

1. **Which statement is true about the following equation?**
   $6,827 \times \dfrac{2}{7} = ?$

   Ⓐ The product will be less than 6,827.
   Ⓑ The product will be greater than 6,827.
   Ⓒ The product will be less than $\dfrac{2}{7}$.
   Ⓓ The product will be equal to $6,827 \div 7$.

2. **Which statement is true about the following equation?**
   $27,093 \times \dfrac{5}{4} = ?$

   Ⓐ The product will be equal to $27,093 \div 54$.
   Ⓑ The product will be less than $\dfrac{5}{4}$.
   Ⓒ The product will be less than 27,093.
   Ⓓ The product will be greater than 27,093.

3. **Estimate the product:**
   $18,612 \times 1\dfrac{1}{7} = $ _____

4. **Which number completes the equation?**
   $3,606 \times \underline{\ \ } = 4,808$
   Enter your answer in the box given below

5. **Which number completes the equation?**
   $\underline{\ \ } \times \dfrac{5}{6} = 17,365$

   Ⓐ 5,838
   Ⓑ 50,838
   Ⓒ 20,838
   Ⓓ 10,838

6. When 6 is multiplied by the following fractions, which of the products will be greater than 6? Select all the correct answers.

(A) $\frac{4}{5}$

(B) $\frac{10}{9}$

(C) $\frac{3}{2}$

(D) $\frac{13}{14}$

7. Write the correct comparison symbol that best completes the statement.

(A) $5 \times \frac{2}{3}$ ☐ 5

(B) $\frac{4}{3} \times 8$ ☐ 8

(C) $12 \times \frac{4}{7}$ ☐ 12

(D) $4 \times \frac{24}{24}$ ☐ 4

8. Which of the following expressions is true.

(A) $25 \times \frac{6}{7} > 25$

(B) $\frac{4}{3} \times 43 < 43$

(C) $\frac{9}{15} \times 16 < 16$

(D) $59 \times \frac{19}{20} > 59$

9. Compare using < , > or =

$$44 \ \square \ 44 \times \frac{3}{4}$$

(A) <

(B) >

(C) =

10. Order the following products from the least to the greatest

$\frac{3}{7}$ x 310, $1\frac{1}{2}$ x 310, $\frac{7}{7}$ x 310

Ⓐ $\frac{3}{7}$ x 310, $\frac{7}{7}$ x 310, $1\frac{1}{2}$ x 310

Ⓑ $1\frac{1}{2}$ x 310, $\frac{7}{7}$ x 310, $\frac{3}{7}$ x 310

Ⓒ $\frac{3}{7}$ x 310, $1\frac{1}{2}$ x 310, $\frac{7}{7}$ x 310

Ⓓ $1\frac{1}{2}$ x 310, $\frac{7}{7}$ x 310, $\frac{3}{7}$ x 310

Chapter 4

Lesson 8: Real World Problems with Fractions

You can scan the QR code given below or use the url to access additional EdSearch resources including videos and mobile apps related to *Real World Problems with Fractions*.

 **Real World Problems with Fractions**

URL	QR Code
http://www.lumoslearning.com/a/5nfb6	

1. Chef Chris is using $\frac{3}{4}$ lb. of chicken per person at a luncheon. If there are 17 people at the luncheon, how many pounds of chicken will he use?

   Ⓐ $12\frac{3}{4}$

   Ⓑ $\frac{51}{68}$

   Ⓒ $\frac{48}{4}$

   Ⓓ $17\frac{3}{4}$

2. A team of runners ran a relay race $\frac{9}{10}$ of a mile long. If Carl ran $\frac{3}{5}$ of the race, how far did his teammates run?

   Ⓐ $\frac{9}{25}$ mile

   Ⓑ $\frac{27}{50}$ mile

   Ⓒ $\frac{1}{10}$ mile

   Ⓓ $\frac{2}{5}$ mile

3. There are $1\frac{4}{5}$ pounds of jelly beans in each bag. If Mrs. Lancer buys 3 bags of jelly beans for her class, how many pounds of jelly beans will she have in all?

   Ⓐ $3\frac{12}{15}$

   Ⓑ $5\frac{2}{5}$

   Ⓒ $3\frac{4}{15}$

   Ⓓ $5\frac{4}{5}$

4. Mario is in a bike race that is $3\frac{1}{5}$ miles long. He gets a flat tire $\frac{2}{3}$ of the way into the race. How many miles did he make it before he got a flat tire?

   Ⓐ $3\frac{2}{15}$

   Ⓑ $1\frac{3}{8}$

   Ⓒ $2\frac{2}{15}$

   Ⓓ $\frac{2}{3}$

5. Jackson is swimming laps in a pool that is $20\frac{1}{2}$ meters long. He swims $4\frac{1}{2}$ laps. How many meters did he swim?

Ⓐ $80\frac{1}{4}$

Ⓑ $92\frac{1}{4}$

Ⓒ $84\frac{1}{2}$

Ⓓ 90

6. A sack of potatoes weighs $4\frac{2}{3}$ lbs. If there are 20 sacks of potatoes in a crate, what is the total weight of the potatoes (in pounds)?

Ⓐ $93\frac{1}{3}$

Ⓑ $80\frac{40}{60}$

Ⓒ $80\frac{2}{3}$

Ⓓ $24\frac{2}{3}$

7. A factory packages bolts that are each $1\frac{1}{8}$ inches wide. If there are 6 bolts side-by-side in a package, how many inches wide must the packaging be?

Ⓐ $6\frac{1}{8}$

Ⓑ $7\frac{5}{8}$

Ⓒ $7\frac{1}{8}$

Ⓓ $6\frac{6}{8}$

8. There are 21 students in a fifth grade class. It takes their teacher $1\frac{1}{4}$ hours to complete each student's report card. How many hours will the report cards take all together?

Ⓐ $24\frac{3}{4}$

Ⓑ $21\frac{1}{4}$

Ⓒ $21\frac{21}{84}$

Ⓓ $26\frac{1}{4}$

9. Kara multiplied some measurements to determine that she needs $\frac{14}{3}$ yards of fabric for a project. How many yards of fabric should she ask for at the store?

Ⓐ $1\frac{4}{3}$

Ⓑ $14\frac{1}{3}$

Ⓒ $4\frac{2}{3}$

Ⓓ $2\frac{1}{3}$

10. Danny needs $5\frac{1}{4}$ feet of tile trim for his kitchen. The tile is sold in pieces that are $\frac{1}{4}$ of a foot long. How many pieces should he buy?

Ⓐ 6

Ⓑ 21

Ⓒ 20

Ⓓ $\frac{5}{16}$

11. Jacobi is making a ramp. If the area of the ramp must be less than 2 m² but more than 1 m² which of the following are possible dimensions of the ramp? Select all the correct answers.

Ⓐ Length = $1\frac{2}{5}$ m; Width = $1\frac{1}{6}$ m

Ⓑ Length = $2\frac{3}{4}$ m; Width = $\frac{7}{8}$ m

Ⓒ Length = $\frac{6}{5}$ m; Width = $\frac{8}{9}$ m

Ⓓ Length = $\frac{3}{7}$ m; Width = $2\frac{4}{5}$ m

12. Kendra ran 6 miles. Her friend Riley ran $\frac{2}{3}$ as far as Kendra. How far did Riley run? Simplify the answer and enter it in the box.

13. Leila is reading a book for school. On Monday she read $\frac{1}{12}$ of the book. On Tuesday she read $\frac{3}{4}$ as much as she read on Monday. What fraction of the book did Leila read on Tuesday? Circle the correct answer.

Ⓐ $\frac{5}{6}$

Ⓑ $\frac{1}{9}$

Ⓒ $\frac{1}{16}$

Ⓓ $\frac{3}{24}$

Chapter 4

Lesson 9: Dividing Fractions

You can scan the QR code given below or use the url to access additional EdSearch resources including videos and mobile apps related to *Dividing Fractions*.

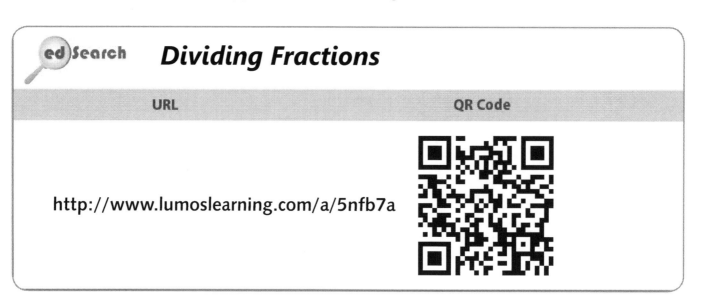

ed Search	Dividing Fractions	
URL		**QR Code**
http://www.lumoslearning.com/a/5nfb7a		

1. **Divide:** $2 \div \dfrac{1}{3} =$

   Ⓐ 3
   Ⓑ 2
   Ⓒ 1
   Ⓓ 6

2. **In order to divide by a fraction you must first:**

   Ⓐ find its reciprocal
   Ⓑ match its denominator
   Ⓒ find its factors
   Ⓓ multiply by the numerator

3. **Divide:** $3 \div \dfrac{2}{3} =$

   Ⓐ $4 \dfrac{2}{3}$
   Ⓑ $3 \dfrac{2}{3}$
   Ⓒ 4
   Ⓓ $4 \dfrac{1}{2}$

4. **Complete the following:**
   Dividing a number by a fraction less than 1 results in a quotient that is _____ the original number.

   Ⓐ the reciprocal of
   Ⓑ less than
   Ⓒ greater than
   Ⓓ equal to

5. **5 people want to evenly share a $\dfrac{1}{3}$ pound bag of peanuts. How many pounds should each person get?**

   Ⓐ $\dfrac{3}{5}$
   Ⓑ $1\dfrac{2}{3}$
   Ⓒ $\dfrac{3}{15}$
   Ⓓ $\dfrac{1}{15}$

6. A jeweler has $\frac{1}{8}$ of a pound of gold. If she uses it to make 4 bracelets, how many pounds of gold will be in each bracelet?

(A) $\frac{2}{16}$

(B) $\frac{1}{32}$

(C) $\frac{1}{4}$

(D) $\frac{4}{8}$

7. Tony is running a long distance race. If he stops for water every $\frac{1}{3}$ mile, how many times will he stop for water in a 10 mile race?

(A) 3.33
(B) 13
(C) 30
(D) 7

8. Which statement proves that $\frac{1}{6} \div 3 = \frac{1}{18}$?

(A) $\frac{3}{18} = \frac{1}{6}$

(B) $\frac{1}{6} \times 3 = \frac{3}{6}$

(C) $\frac{1}{18} \div 3 = \frac{1}{6}$

(D) $\frac{1}{18} \times 3 = \frac{3}{18}$

9. Dividing a fraction by a whole number makes it _____.

(A) smaller
(B) larger
(C) change to its reciprocal
(D) improper

10. The scout leader bought an 8 pound bag of trail mix. If he divides it into $\frac{1}{4}$ pound servings, how many servings will there be?

   Ⓐ 20
   Ⓑ 32
   Ⓒ 4
   Ⓓ 18

11. Which statement proves that $10 \div \frac{1}{4} = 40$?
   Circle the correct answer

   Ⓐ $\frac{1}{40} \times 10 = \frac{10}{40}$

   Ⓑ $\frac{1}{4} \times \frac{1}{10} = \frac{1}{40}$

   Ⓒ $40 \times \frac{1}{4} = 10$

   Ⓓ $4 \times 10 = 40$

12. Read each equation below and mark whether the equation is true or false.

	True	False
$6 \div \frac{1}{3} > 16$	○	○
$\frac{1}{4} \div 3 = \frac{3}{12}$	○	○
$12 \div \frac{1}{6} < 80$	○	○
$\frac{1}{5} \div 2 > 9$	○	○

13. What four unit fractions complete the equations below? Enter your answers in the table.

2	÷		=	12
	÷	5	=	$\frac{1}{15}$
12	÷		=	48
	÷	4	=	$\frac{1}{28}$

Chapter 4

Lesson 10: Dividing by Unit Fractions

You can scan the QR code given below or use the url to access additional EdSearch resources including videos and mobile apps related to *Dividing by Unit Fractions*.

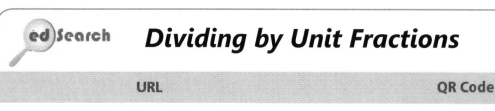

URL	QR Code
http://www.lumoslearning.com/a/5nfb7b	

LumosLearning.com

1. Which best explains why $6 \div \dfrac{1}{4} = 24$?

Ⓐ $24 \div \dfrac{1}{4} = 6$

Ⓑ $24 \times \dfrac{1}{4} = 6$

Ⓒ $24 \div 6 = \dfrac{1}{4}$

Ⓓ $24 = \dfrac{1}{4} \times 6$

2. Which model best represents the following equation?
$4 \div \dfrac{1}{3} = 12$

Ⓐ

Ⓑ

Ⓒ

Ⓓ

3. Which equation matches this model?

Ⓐ $24 \div \dfrac{1}{8} = 3$

Ⓑ $24 \div \dfrac{1}{3} = 8$

Ⓒ $8 \div \dfrac{1}{3} = 24$

Ⓓ $3 \div \dfrac{1}{8} = 24$

4. **Byron has 5 pieces of wood from which to build his birdhouse. If he cuts each piece into fifths, how many pieces will he have?**

Ⓐ 25

Ⓑ 5

Ⓒ $\dfrac{1}{5}$

Ⓓ $\dfrac{5}{25}$

5. **Angelina has 10 yards of fabric. She needs $\dfrac{1}{3}$ yard of fabric for each purse she will sew. How many purses will she be able to make?**

Ⓐ $3\dfrac{1}{3}$

Ⓑ $10\dfrac{1}{3}$

Ⓒ 30

Ⓓ 13

6. **What is the value of 4 divided by $\dfrac{1}{5}$. Circle the correct answer choice.**

Ⓐ $\dfrac{4}{5}$

Ⓑ 20

Ⓒ $\dfrac{1}{20}$

Ⓓ 9

7. **Read each statement below and indicate whether it is true or false.**

Statements	True	False
$\dfrac{1}{12} \div 4 > 40$	○	○
$\dfrac{1}{4} \div 7 = \dfrac{1}{14}$	○	○
$\dfrac{1}{3} \div 33 < 5$	○	○
$\dfrac{1}{8} \div 4 < \dfrac{1}{2}$	○	○

8. **What three unit fractions complete the equations below? Enter your answers into the table.**

	÷	14	=	$\frac{1}{112}$
	÷	29	=	$\frac{1}{87}$
	÷	55	=	$\frac{1}{495}$

9. Evaluate $8 \div \frac{1}{3}$.

   (A) 24
   (B) 27
   (C) 21
   (D) 2.7

10. Evaluate $4 \div \frac{7}{21}$.

   (A) 7
   (B) 12
   (C) 27
   (D) 36

Chapter 4

Lesson 11: Real World Problems Dividing Fractions

You can scan the QR code given below or use the url to access additional EdSearch resources including videos and mobile apps related to *Real World Problems* Dividing Fractions.

 **Real World Problems Dividing Fractions**

URL	QR Code
http://www.lumoslearning.com/a/5nfb7c	

1. Darren has a 3 cup bag of snack mix. Each serving is $\frac{1}{4}$ cup. Which model will help him determine how many $\frac{1}{4}$ cup servings are in the whole bag of snack mix?

Ⓐ

Ⓑ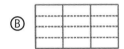

Ⓒ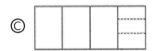

Ⓓ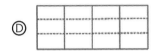

2. Which situation could be represented by the following model?

Ⓐ The number of $\frac{1}{8}$ lb. servings of cheese in 4 lbs. of cheese

Ⓑ Four friends share 8 lbs. of cheese

Ⓒ 4 lbs. of cheese divided into 8 equal servings

Ⓓ The amount of cheese needed for 8 people to each have $\frac{1}{4}$ lb.

3. A team of 3 runners competes in a $\frac{1}{4}$ mile relay race. If each person runs an equal portion of the race, how far does each person run?

Ⓐ $\frac{3}{7}$ mile

Ⓑ $\frac{3}{12}$ mile

Ⓒ $\frac{3}{4}$ mile

Ⓓ $\frac{1}{12}$ mile

4. A beaker holds $\frac{1}{10}$ of a liter of water. If the water is divided equally into 6 test tubes, how much water will be in each test tube?

Ⓐ $\frac{1}{60}$ liter

Ⓑ $\frac{6}{10}$ liter

Ⓒ $\frac{1}{6}$ liter

Ⓓ $\frac{10}{16}$

5. Mrs. Blake orders 3 pizzas for a school party. If each slice is $\frac{1}{12}$ of a pizza, how many slices are there in all?

Ⓐ 24

Ⓑ $4\frac{1}{3}$

Ⓒ 36

Ⓓ $\frac{3}{12}$

6. Lawson, Rhett and Wynn bought packages of silly putty. Lawson divided each of his five packages into thirds, Rhett divided each of his four packages into fourths and Wynn divided each of his 3 packages into fifths. Based on this information, which of the following two statements are true?

Ⓐ Lawson and Wynn have the same number of portions of silly putty.

Ⓑ Wynn has five more portions of silly putty than Rhett.

Ⓒ Rhett has more portions of silly putty than Lawson.

Ⓓ Lawson, Rhett and Wynn all have the same number of portions of silly putty.

7. Mrs. Klein has a small rectangular area in her backyard to use for composting. If the width of the rectangular area is $1\frac{1}{7}$ yards and the compost area must be less than 6 square yards, what is the maximum length of the garden?
Enter your answer in the box below.

8. The basketball coach advised all players to drink 2500 milliliters of water during the day before each game. How much is this in liters?

Ⓐ 0.25 liters
Ⓑ 2.5 liters
Ⓒ 25 liters
Ⓓ 250 liters

9. Sam is painting his house. If he needs $\frac{1}{2}$ liter of paint per room. How many liters of paint is required to paint 4 rooms?

Ⓐ 2 liters
Ⓑ 3 liters
Ⓒ 4 liters
Ⓓ 5 liters

10. Mathew has $\frac{4}{5}$ of a tank of fuel in his car. He needs 1/10 of a tank per day. How many days will the fuel in his tank last?

Ⓐ 6 days
Ⓑ 8 days
Ⓒ 5 days
Ⓓ 7 days

End of Numbers and Operations – Fractions

Chapter 4:

Numbers and Operations – Fractions

Answer Key
&
Detailed Explanations

Lesson 1: Add & Subtract Fractions

Question No.	Answer	Detailed Explanations
1	B	When fractions have a common denominator (in this case 10), just add the numerators (2 + 1 = 3) and keep the denominator the same.
2	A	Add the whole numbers (1+1) to get 2. Then add the fractions. As they have a common denominator of 4, just add the numerators (1+2) to get $\frac{3}{4}$. The total is $2\frac{3}{4}$.
3	B	As the fractions have a common denominator of 4, just subtract the numerators (3 - 2) to get $\frac{1}{4}$.
4	D	Subtract the whole numbers (3 - 1) to get 2. Then subtract the fractions. Since they have a common denominator of 10, just subtract the numerators (4 - 1) to get $\frac{3}{10}$. The total is $2\frac{3}{10}$.
5	D	Fractions must have a common denominator to be added. Multiply both the numerator and the denominator by 3 to get $\frac{9}{12}$ so that both the fractions have a common denominator 12.
6	C	Fractions must have a common denominator to be added. Multiply both the numerator and the denominator by 2 to get $\frac{2}{4}$. Then add the numerators (2+1) to get the numerator of the sum and keep the common denominator 4, to get the sum, $\frac{3}{4}$.
7	B	For subtracting fractions (proper or improper), find the common denominator and find the equivalent fractions in terms of this common denominator and subtract them. Then, write the fraction in its simplest form. $\frac{2}{3} = \frac{2\times3}{3\times3} = \frac{6}{9}$ $\frac{2}{3} - \frac{1}{9} = \frac{6}{9} - \frac{1}{9} = \frac{6-1}{9} = \frac{5}{9}$.
8	D	First add the whole numbers (2 + 5) to get 7. Then add the fraction parts. Since fractions must have a common denominator to be added, find the equivalent fractions in terms of the common denominator and add them. $\frac{1}{2} \times \frac{1\times4}{2\times4} = \frac{4}{8}$. $\frac{1}{8} + \frac{1}{2} = \frac{1}{8} + \frac{4}{8} = \frac{1+4}{8} = \frac{5}{8}$. The total is $7\frac{5}{8}$.

Question No.	Answer	Detailed Explanations
9	A	First add the whole numbers (5 + 1) to get 6. Then add the fraction parts. Since fractions must have a common denominator to be added, find the equivalent fractions in terms of the common denominator and add them. $\frac{1}{4} = \frac{1 \times 2}{4 \times 2} = \frac{2}{8}$ $\frac{5}{8} + \frac{1}{4} = \frac{5}{8} + \frac{2}{8} = \frac{5+2}{8} = \frac{7}{8}$ The total is $6\frac{7}{8}$.
10	D	In order to subtract a fraction from a whole number, convert 1 from the whole number into a fraction with a common denominator. The number 1 can be converted to thirds by changing it to $\frac{3}{3}$. That leaves $4\frac{3}{3} - \frac{1}{3}$. Keep 4 as the whole number & subtract the numerators of the fractions to get $\frac{2}{3}$.
11	C	Subtract the whole numbers (8 - 2) to get 6. Then subtract the fractions. Since they have a common denominator of 16, just subtract the numerators (5 - 3) to get $\frac{2}{16}$. The total is $6\frac{2}{16}$.
12	D	To find the amount of growth of hair subtract $8\frac{1}{2}$ inches from $10\frac{3}{4}$ inches. $10\frac{3}{4} - 8\frac{1}{2} = (10-8) + (\frac{3}{4} - \frac{1}{2})$ Since $\frac{1}{2}$ and $\frac{3}{4}$ do not have a common denominator, multiply both the numerator and the denominator of $\frac{1}{2}$ by 2 to get $\frac{2}{4}$. $\frac{1}{2} = \frac{1 \times 2}{2 \times 2} = \frac{2}{4}$ $\frac{3}{4} - \frac{1}{2} = \frac{3}{4} - \frac{2}{4} = \frac{3-2}{4} = \frac{1}{4}$ $10\frac{3}{4} - 8\frac{1}{2} = (10-8) + (\frac{3}{4} - \frac{1}{2}) = 2 + \frac{1}{4} = 2\frac{1}{4}$ inches.
13	$1\frac{3}{5}$	Since the fractions all have a common denominator (5), just add the numerators. 1 + 3 + 4 = 8, keep the common denominator 5 to get sum $\frac{8}{5}$. Convert $\frac{8}{5}$ into mixed fraction. $\frac{8}{5} = 1\frac{3}{5}$.

Question No.	Answer	Detailed Explanations
14	A	Since this is a missing added problem, it can be solved by subtracting $4\frac{1}{4}$ from $7\frac{1}{2}$. First, subtract the whole numbers (7-4) to get 3. Then subtract the fractions. Since $\frac{1}{2}$ and $\frac{1}{4}$ do not have a common denominator, multiply both the numerator and the denominator of $\frac{1}{2}$ by 2 to get $\frac{2}{4}$. $\frac{1}{2} = \frac{1\times2}{2\times2} = \frac{2}{4}$ $\frac{1}{2} - \frac{1}{4} = \frac{2}{4} - \frac{1}{4} = \frac{2-1}{4} = \frac{1}{4}$ $7\frac{1}{2} - 4\frac{1}{4} = (7-4) + (\frac{1}{2}-\frac{1}{4}) = 3 + \frac{1}{4} = 3\frac{1}{4}$
15	B	First, complete the part of the problem in parentheses. As the fractions have a common denominator (10), just subtract the numerators to get $\frac{3}{10}$. Then subtract the $\frac{3}{10}$ from $\frac{7}{10}$ to get $\frac{4}{10}$.
16	B & C	When adding fractions, first get a common denominator. The common denominators of 3 and 4 are multiples of 12 : 12, 24, 36, 48, 60.... This eliminates answer choices A and D, since 6 and 16 are not common denominators of 3 and 4. To get an equivalent fraction, multiply both the numerator and denominator by the same number. (B) $\frac{2}{3} = \frac{(2\times4)}{(3\times4)} = \frac{8}{12}$; $\frac{7}{4} = \frac{(7\times3)}{(4\times3)} = \frac{21}{12}$ Therefore, $\frac{8}{12} + \frac{21}{12}$ is an equivalent expression. (C) $\frac{2}{3} = \frac{(2\times20)}{(3\times20)} = \frac{40}{60}$; $\frac{7}{4} = \frac{(7\times15)}{(4\times15)} = \frac{105}{60}$ Therefore, $\frac{40}{60} + \frac{105}{60}$ is an equivalent expression. (E) $\frac{2}{3} = \frac{(2\times12)}{(3\times12)} = \frac{24}{36}$; $\frac{7}{4} = \frac{(7\times9)}{(4\times9)} = \frac{63}{36}$ Therefore, $\frac{20}{36} + \frac{54}{36}$ is NOT an equivalent expression.
17	$\frac{11}{35}$	When subtracting fractions, first get a common denominator. The lowest common denominator of 5 and 7 is 5 X 7 = 35. Write an equivalent expression with denominators of 35 and subtract numerators. $\frac{3}{5} - \frac{2}{7} = \frac{21}{35} - \frac{10}{35} = \frac{11}{35}$

Lesson 2: Problem Solving with Fractions

Question No.	Answer	Detailed Explanations
1	C	Multiply 60 (the number of minutes in an hour) by $\frac{3}{4}$ to find the number of minutes she practiced. $60 \times \frac{3}{4} = \frac{180}{4} = 45$
2	A	Multiply 30 by $\frac{3}{5}$ to find the number of boys. $30 \times \frac{3}{5} = \frac{90}{5} = 18$ If there are 18 boys, there must be 12 girls (30 - 18 = 12).
3	D	To solve, divide 11 miles by 3 hours. Convert the improper fraction to a mixed number. $\frac{11}{3} = 3\frac{2}{3}$
4	D	A whole apple is 1, or $\frac{8}{8}$. To find out how much is not water, subtract the fraction that is water. $\frac{8}{8} - \frac{7}{8} = \frac{1}{8}$
5	C	This problem has a lot of extra information. To find the number of pumpkins that were too small, just multiply the total number of pumpkins (20) by the fraction of pumpkins that were too small $(\frac{1}{4})$. $20 \times \frac{1}{4} = \frac{20}{4} = 5$ Convert from an improper fraction to a whole number by dividing 20 by 4.
6	A	Timothy gave away 9 out of 45 shirts. This is the fraction $\frac{9}{45}$. Since that option is not available, reduce the fraction to lowest terms by dividing both the numerator and denominator by 9. $\frac{9}{45} = \frac{9}{9} \div \frac{45}{9} = \frac{1}{5}$

Question No.	Answer	Detailed Explanations
7	B	4 out of 32 students come to tutoring. This is the fraction $\frac{4}{32}$. Since that option is not available, reduce the fraction by dividing both the numerator and the denominator by 4. $\frac{4}{32} = (\frac{4}{4}) \div \frac{32}{4}) = \frac{1}{8}$
8	B	She has completed $\frac{14}{35}$ problems. This means she has 21 left to do (35 - 14 = 21). 21 out of 35 is the fraction $\frac{21}{35}$. Since that option is not available, reduce the fraction by dividing both the numerator and denominator by 7. $\frac{21}{35} = (\frac{21}{7}) \div (\frac{35}{7}) = \frac{3}{5}$
9	D	Multiply 32 by $\frac{2}{8}$ to find the number of points they scored in the second half. $32 \times \frac{2}{8} = \frac{64}{8} = 8$ If they scored 8 points in the second half, they must have scored 24 points in the first half (32 - 8 = 24).
10	C	You will only need half the amount of flour, since 24 is half of 48. Multiply 3 cups by $\frac{1}{2}$ to find out how much flour to use. $3 \times \frac{1}{2} = \frac{3}{2} = 1\frac{1}{2}$

11

	>	<	=
$\dfrac{5}{6} - \dfrac{2}{3} \ \square \ \dfrac{1}{2} - \dfrac{3}{8}$	◯		
$\dfrac{5}{6} + \dfrac{2}{3} \ \square \ \dfrac{3}{4} + \dfrac{5}{12}$	◯		
$\dfrac{3}{15} + \dfrac{2}{5} \ \square \ \dfrac{1}{3} + \dfrac{2}{5}$		◯	
$\dfrac{7}{8} - \dfrac{1}{4} \ \square \ \dfrac{3}{4} - \dfrac{1}{8}$			◯

When adding or subtracting fractions first get a common denominator, then add or subtract the numerators and simplify the answer. When comparing fractions get a common denominator and compare numerators.

$$\dfrac{5}{6} - \dfrac{2}{3} = \dfrac{5}{6} - \dfrac{4}{6} = \dfrac{1}{6}; \qquad \dfrac{1}{2} - \dfrac{3}{8} = \dfrac{4}{8} - \dfrac{3}{8} = \dfrac{1}{8}$$

$$\rightarrow \dfrac{1}{6} > \dfrac{1}{8} \text{ because } \dfrac{8}{48} > \dfrac{6}{48}$$

$$\dfrac{5}{6} + \dfrac{2}{3} = \dfrac{5}{6} + \dfrac{4}{6} = \dfrac{9}{6} = \dfrac{3}{2}; \qquad \dfrac{3}{4} + \dfrac{5}{12} = \dfrac{9}{12} + \dfrac{5}{12} = \dfrac{14}{12} = \dfrac{7}{6}$$

$$\rightarrow \dfrac{3}{2} > \dfrac{7}{6} \text{ because } \dfrac{9}{6} > \dfrac{7}{6}$$

$$\dfrac{3}{15} + \dfrac{2}{5} = \dfrac{3}{15} + \dfrac{6}{15} = \dfrac{9}{15} = \dfrac{3}{5}; \qquad \dfrac{1}{3} + \dfrac{3}{5} = \dfrac{5}{15} + \dfrac{9}{15} = \dfrac{14}{15}$$

$$\rightarrow \dfrac{3}{5} < \dfrac{14}{15} \text{ because } \dfrac{9}{15} > \dfrac{14}{15}$$

$$\dfrac{7}{8} - \dfrac{1}{4} = \dfrac{7}{8} - \dfrac{2}{8} = \dfrac{5}{8}; \qquad \dfrac{3}{4} - \dfrac{1}{8} = \dfrac{6}{8} - \dfrac{1}{8} = \dfrac{5}{8} \qquad \rightarrow \dfrac{5}{8} = \dfrac{5}{8}$$

12   **A**

To find the amount of butter remaining, subtract $\dfrac{1}{2}$ from $\dfrac{5}{8}$. When subtracting fraction, get a common denominator, subtract numerators and simplify the answer.

$$\dfrac{5}{8} - \dfrac{1}{2} = \dfrac{5}{8} - \dfrac{4}{8} = \dfrac{1}{8}$$

A is the correct answer choice.

Question No.	Answer	Detailed Explanations
13	B	To determine the amount of paint used, we have to add $\frac{2}{3}$ and $\frac{2}{15}$. When adding fractions, first find a common denominator, add the numerators and simplify the answer. $$\frac{2}{3} + \frac{2}{5} = \frac{10}{15} + \frac{2}{15} = \frac{12}{15} = \frac{4}{5}$$ B is the correct answer choice.

Lesson 3: Interpreting Fractions

Question No.	Answer	Detailed Explanations
1	A	The first three cookies can be shared by having each friend receive 1 whole cookie. That leaves 1 cookie to be divided among the three friends. This can be shown as a fraction with the dividend (1) as the numerator and the divisor (3) as the denominator. Each friend will receive 1 whole cookie and $\frac{1}{3}$ of the last cookie that was divided.
2	B	The number 5 goes into 18 three whole times (5 x 3 = 15), leaving a remainder of 3. That three can be divided by 5 to get the required fraction, $\frac{3}{5}$.
3	B	To solve, divide 90 minutes by 4 squads. This creates the improper fraction $\frac{90}{4}$. To change it to a mixed number, divide 90 by 4 to get 22 remainder 2. The remainder of 2 also needs to be divided among the 4 squads, so it becomes the fraction $\frac{2}{4}$, or $\frac{1}{2}$. Each squad will play for $22\frac{1}{2}$ minutes.
4	D	To find $\frac{2}{5}$ of 695, multiply the whole number by the fraction. Since $\frac{2}{5}$ is really 2 ÷ 5, this means you will multiply 695 x 2 ÷ 5.
5	C	7 hours divided by 5 people is the fraction $\frac{7}{5}$. Of this, $\frac{5}{5}$ equals one whole, leaving $\frac{2}{5}$ as a fraction. These $\frac{2}{5}$ are not 2 minutes, they are a fraction of an hour. The total time is $1\frac{2}{5}$.
6	D	A fraction is the division of the numerator by the denominator. The fraction $\frac{3}{10}$ is equivalent to 3 ÷ 10.
7	C	A fraction is the division of the numerator by the denominator.
8	B	The division of two whole numbers (such as 1 cake divided by 9 people) can be shown as a fraction with the dividend as the numerator and the divisor as the denominator.
9	A	A fraction is the division of the numerator by the denominator. The fraction $\frac{4}{7}$ is equivalent to 4÷7. Therefore, $\frac{4}{7}$ x 7 = $\frac{4 \times 7}{7}$ = $\frac{28}{7}$ = 4.
10	C	A fraction is the division of the numerator by the denominator. The fraction $\frac{2}{3}$ is equivalent to 2 ÷ 3.

Question No.	Answer	Detailed Explanations
11	B & C	A fraction states the number of parts as the numerator and the total number of parts in the whole as the denominator. Since Sinclair made six points out of the total of twenty-four points he made $\frac{6}{24} = \frac{1}{4}$ of the total. Answer choices B and C are correct.
12	$\frac{3}{4}$	Divide 6-feet by 8 or write $\frac{6}{8}$. Then simplify the fraction $$\frac{6}{8} = \frac{\frac{6}{2}}{\frac{8}{2}} = \frac{3}{4}$$ Therefore each bracelet was $\frac{3}{4}$-feet long.

Lesson 4: Multiply Fractions

Question No.	Answer	Detailed Explanations
1	A	First, multiply the numerators (2 x 4 = 8) then multiply the denominators (3 x 5 = 15) to get the fraction $\frac{8}{15}$.
2	D	Multiply the first two terms first, using $\frac{5}{1}$ for the whole number 5. $\frac{5}{1} \times \frac{2}{3} = \frac{10}{3}$. Then multiply this fraction by the third term: $\frac{10}{3} \times \frac{1}{2} = \frac{10}{6}$ Change the improper fraction $\frac{10}{6}$ to a mixed number by dividing 10 by 6. Then change $1\frac{4}{6}$ into lowest terms, which is $1\frac{2}{3}$.
3	B	Multiplying a fraction by a whole number is the same as multiplying the numerator by a whole number then dividing the product by the denominator.
4	C	The product of two fractions is equal to the product of the numerators divided by the product of the denominators.
5	B	To solve, multiply $\frac{4}{7} \times \frac{3}{5} \times 4$. Multiply the first two terms first: $\frac{4}{7} \times \frac{3}{5} = \frac{12}{35}$ Then multiply this fraction by 4. Remember that the whole number 4 can be shown as the fraction $\frac{4}{1}$. $\frac{12}{35} \times 4 = \frac{48}{35}$ Since $\frac{35}{35}$ is 1 whole the fraction can be shown as the mixed number $1\frac{13}{35}$.
6	C	Multiply 600 by $\frac{1}{3}$ to find the number of seats that are empty. $\frac{600}{1} \times \frac{1}{3} = \frac{600}{3} = 200$
7	C	Three of the options represent 5 whole units and a fractional half. $\frac{25}{50}$ is equivalent to one half and so is 0.500. The improper fraction $\frac{44}{8}$ can be changed to a mixed number by dividing 44 by 8 to get $5\frac{4}{8}$ (which is equal to $5\frac{1}{2}$). The fraction $5\frac{1}{5}$ is not equivalent to the other three.

Question No.	Answer	Detailed Explanations
8	B	Multiply the numerators (1 x 1 = 1) then multiply the denominators (2 x 4 = 8) to get the fraction $\frac{1}{8}$.
9	C	To solve, multiply $\frac{1}{2}$ x $\frac{3}{4}$. First, multiply the numerators (1 x 3 = 3) then multiply the denominators (2 x 4 = 8) to get the fraction $\frac{3}{8}$.
10	B	To solve, multiply $\frac{1}{2}$ x $\frac{1}{10}$. First, multiply the numerators (1 x 1 = 1) then multiply the denominators (2 x 10 = 20) to get the fraction $\frac{1}{20}$.

11

	True	False
$4 \times \dfrac{3}{4} = 3$	●	○
$\dfrac{1}{6}$ of 7 is $\dfrac{6}{7}$	○	●
$\dfrac{1}{3} \times 9 = 3$	●	○
$10 \times \dfrac{1}{6} = 1\dfrac{2}{3}$	●	○

When multiplying a whole number by a fraction, rewrite the whole number as a fraction with a denominator of 1. Then multiply the numerators and denominators. Finally, simplify the answer to a fraction in simplest form or a mixed number.

$$4 \times \frac{3}{4} = \frac{4}{1} \times \frac{3}{4} = \frac{12}{4} = 3$$

$$\frac{1}{6} \times 7 = \frac{1}{6} \times \frac{7}{1} = \frac{7}{6} = 1\frac{1}{6}$$

$$\frac{1}{3} \times 9 = \frac{1}{3} \times \frac{9}{1} = \frac{9}{3} = 3$$

$$10 \times \frac{1}{6} = \frac{10}{1} \times \frac{1}{6} = \frac{10}{6} = 1\frac{4}{6} = 1\frac{2}{3}$$

12		When multiplying fractions, multiply numerators and put them over the product of the denominators. Then simplify the fraction.

$\dfrac{1}{6}$	×	$\dfrac{3}{4}$	=	$\dfrac{3}{24}$	=	$\dfrac{1}{8}$

13	A	Each of three people received $\dfrac{1}{6}$ pound of chocolate. Therefore Terry brought $3 \times \dfrac{1}{6} = \dfrac{3}{6}$ pound of chocolate. This is best represented by the model in the first box.

Lesson 5: Multiply to Find Area

Question No.	Answer	Detailed Explanations
1	A	Find the area of the desk top by multiplying: $\frac{7}{8}$ yd x $\frac{3}{4}$ yd = $\frac{21}{32}$ yd²
2	C	Find the area of the floor by multiplying: $2\frac{1}{2}$ x $3\frac{3}{4}$ = $\frac{5}{2}$ x $\frac{15}{4}$ = $\frac{75}{8}$ = $9\frac{3}{8}$
3	D	Multiplying length x width of a rectangle and tiling the rectangle with unit squares are both accurate ways to determine area. Therefore, Lin and Tyra should both end up with the same answer, or nearly the same answer (since counting fractional parts of tiles isn't as precise as multiplying).
4	A	Multiplying length x width of a rectangle should produce the same number as filling the rectangle with unit squares. Therefore, multiply to find that $3\frac{1}{2}$ x 4 = $\frac{7}{2}$ x 4 = $\frac{7 \times 4}{2}$ = $\frac{28}{2}$ = 14
5	B	Find the area of the court by multiplying: $3\frac{1}{3}$ x $5\frac{2}{3}$ = $\frac{10}{3}$ x $\frac{17}{3}$ = $\frac{170}{9}$ = $18\frac{8}{9}$ yd²

Question No.	Answer	Detailed Explanations
6	B & D	To find the area of a rectangle, multiply the length by the width. When multiplying fractions, multiply the numerators together and put it over the product of the denominators. Then simplify the result. Area - $\dfrac{3}{5} \times \dfrac{4}{9} = \dfrac{3 \times 4}{5 \times 9} = \dfrac{12}{45} = \dfrac{\overset{12}{\cancel{3}}}{\underset{3}{\cancel{45}}} = \dfrac{4}{15}$ The correct answer choices are B and D.
7	$1\dfrac{2}{3}$	The area of a rectangle is equal to the length multiplied by the width. Area $= 2 \times \dfrac{5}{6} = \dfrac{2}{1} \times \dfrac{5}{6} = \dfrac{2 \times 5}{1 \times 6} = \dfrac{10}{6} = \dfrac{\overset{10}{\cancel{2}}}{\underset{2}{\cancel{6}}} = \dfrac{5}{3} = 1\dfrac{2}{3}$
8	C	Find the area of each answer choice and compare it to 1 m². When multiplying fraction and mixed numbers, rewrite the mixed number as an improper fraction, multiple the numerators and put this result over the product of the denominators, then simplify. $1\dfrac{3}{8} \times \dfrac{7}{9} = \dfrac{11}{8} \times \dfrac{7}{9} = \dfrac{77}{72} = 1\dfrac{5}{72}$ m² which is greater than 1 m² $2\dfrac{1}{6} \times \dfrac{3}{4} = \dfrac{13}{6} \times \dfrac{3}{4} = \dfrac{39}{24} = 1\dfrac{15}{24}$ m² which is greater than 1 m² $2\dfrac{5}{6} \times \dfrac{1}{3} = \dfrac{17}{6} \times \dfrac{1}{3} = \dfrac{17}{18}$ m² which is less than 1 m² $1\dfrac{7}{8} \times \dfrac{4}{5} = \dfrac{15}{8} \times \dfrac{4}{5} = \dfrac{60}{40} = \dfrac{3}{2} = 1\dfrac{1}{2}$ m² which is greater than 1 m²
9	$\dfrac{3}{8}$	To find the area, we need to multiply $\dfrac{1}{2} \times \dfrac{3}{4} = \dfrac{3}{8}$. The answer choice B is the correct answer.
10	A	The numerator has to be multiplied with the numerator and the denominator needs to be multiplied with the denominator to get the correct answer The correct answer is $\dfrac{7}{24}$ which is answer choice A.

Lesson 6: Multiplication as Scaling

Question No.	Answer	Detailed Explanations
1	A	When multiplying two numbers (a and b), the product will be 'a' times as much as 'b' or 'b' times as much as 'a'.
2	C	When multiplying, if one factor is a fraction greater than 1, the product will be greater than the other factor.
3	B	When multiplying, if one factor is a fraction less than 1, the product will be less than the other factor.
4	D	When multiplying, if one factor is a fraction less than 1, the product will be less than the other factor.
5	C	If Ryan has $\frac{1}{5}$ as many beads as Alex, then Alex has five times as many beads as Ryan. The way to show this is by multiplying Ryan's beads by 5 to equal Alex's beads.
6	D	When multiplying two numbers (a and b), the product will be a times as much as b or b times as much as a.
7	A	When multiplying two numbers (a and b), the product will be a times as much as b or b times as much as a.
8	C	When multiplying two numbers (a and b), the product will be a times as much as b or b times as much as a.
9	A	When multiplying two numbers (a and b), the product will be a times as much as b or b times as much as a.
10	B	When multiplying two numbers (a and b), the product will be a times as much as b or b times as much as a.

11

A number multiplied by a fraction less than one will result in a number less than itself.

A. Since $\frac{3}{4}$ is less than one, $\frac{7}{8} \times \frac{3}{4}$ is less than . Therefore $\frac{7}{8} \times \frac{3}{4} > \frac{7}{8}$ is a false statement.

B. Since $\frac{6}{5}$ is greater than one, $2\frac{1}{2} \times \frac{6}{5}$ is greater than $2\frac{1}{2}$. Therefore $2\frac{1}{2} \times \frac{6}{5} < 2\frac{1}{2}$ is a false statement.

C. Since $\frac{8}{15}$ is less than one, $\frac{8}{15} \times \frac{1}{3}$ is less than $\frac{1}{3}$. Therefore $\frac{8}{15} \times \frac{1}{3} < \frac{1}{3}$ is a true statement.

D. Since $\frac{3}{2}$ is greater than one, $\frac{11}{12} \times \frac{3}{2}$ is greater than $\frac{11}{12}$. Therefore $\frac{11}{12} \times \frac{3}{2} < \frac{11}{12}$ is a false statement.

	True	False
$\frac{7}{8} \times \frac{3}{4} > \frac{7}{8}$	○	◉
$2\frac{1}{2} \times \frac{6}{5} < 2\frac{1}{2}$	○	◉
$\frac{8}{15} \times \frac{1}{3} < \frac{1}{3}$	◉	○
$\frac{11}{12} \times \frac{3}{2} < \frac{11}{12}$	○	◉

12   C

A number multiplied by a fraction greater than one will result in a value greater than the original number. The fractions $\frac{2}{3}, \frac{7}{8}$ and $\frac{3}{4}$ are all less than one. The fraction $\frac{6}{5}$ which can also be written as $1\frac{1}{5}$, is greater than one and thus when multiplies by 3 will result in a number greater than 3.

13

$\dfrac{8}{9}$	×	<1	<	$\dfrac{8}{9}$
<1	×	$1\dfrac{1}{5}$	<	$1\dfrac{1}{5}$
$\dfrac{5}{4}$	×	>1	>	$\dfrac{5}{4}$

A whole number or fraction multiplied by a fraction less than one results in a value less than the original number. A whole number or fraction multiplied by a fraction greater than one results in a value greater than the original number.

A. Since the result is a number less than $\dfrac{8}{9}$, the fraction entered must be less than one.

B. Since the result is a number less than $1\dfrac{1}{5}$, the fraction entered must be less than one.

C. Since the result is a number greater than $\dfrac{5}{4}$, the fraction entered must be greater than one.

Lesson 7: Numbers Multiplied by Fractions

Question No.	Answer	Detailed Explanations
1	A	Multiplying a number by a fraction less than 1 will result in a product that is less than the original number.
2	D	Multiplying a number by a fraction greater than 1 will result in a product that is greater than the original number.
3		Multiplying a number by a fraction greater than 1 will result in a product that is greater than the original number. Since the second factor is only $\frac{1}{7}$ more than one, the product will be just slightly greater than 18,612. $18,612 \times \frac{1}{7} = 21,270.86$
4	$\frac{4}{3}$	Multiplying a number by a fraction greater than 1 will result in a product that is greater than the original number. Since the product is only slightly greater than the original number, the other factor will be just slightly greater than 1. Therefore, $\frac{4}{3}$ (which is equal to $1\frac{1}{3}$) is the only option possible.
5	C	Multiplying a number by a fraction less than 1 will result in a product that is less than the original number. Since the fraction is only slightly less than 1, the other factor will be just slightly greater than 17,365. Therefore, 20,838 is the only option possible, as 50,838 is more than double the product.
6	B & C	When multiplying a whole number by a fraction, if the fraction is less than one, the product will be less than the whole number. If the fraction is greater than one, the product will be greater than the whole number. The fractions that are greater than one are $\frac{10}{9}$ and $\frac{3}{2}$. Therefore 6 times either of these fractions will result in a product greater than 6. The correct answer choices are B and C.

Question No.	Answer	Detailed Explanations
7		When multiplying a whole number by a fraction, if the fraction is less than one, the product will be less than < the whole number. if the fraction is greater than one, the product will be greater than the whole number. Since $\frac{2}{3}$ is less than 1, $5 \times \frac{2}{3} < 5$ Since $\frac{4}{3}$ is greater than 1, $\frac{4}{3} \times 8 > 8$ Since $\frac{4}{7}$ is less than 1, $12 \times \frac{4}{7} < 12$ Since $\frac{24}{24}$ is equal to 1, $4 \times \frac{24}{24} = 4$
8	C	When multiplying a whole number by a fraction, if the fraction is less than one, the product will be less than the whole number. If the fraction is greater than one, the product will be greater than the whole number. Since $\frac{9}{15}$ is less than 1, $\frac{9}{15} \times 16 < 16$. Therefore $\frac{9}{15} \times 16 < 16$ is a true statement.
9	B	$44 \times \frac{3}{4} = 11 \times 3 = 33$ $44 > 33$ The choice B is the correct answer.
10	A	$\frac{3}{7} \times 310$ will be less than 310 $\frac{7}{7} \times 310$ will be 310 since $\frac{7}{7}$ is 1 $1\frac{1}{2} \times 310$ will be greater than 310 The choice A is the correct answer.

Lesson 8: Real World Problems with Fractions

Question No.	Answer	Detailed Explanations
1	A	To multiply a whole number by a fraction, represent the whole number as $\frac{17}{1}$. Then, multiply numerators ($17 \times 3 = 51$) to find the numerator and multiply denominators ($1 \times 4 = 4$) to find the denominator. Change the improper fraction $\frac{51}{4}$ to a mixed number by dividing 51 by 4 to equal $12\frac{3}{4}$.
2	A	To find how far the teammates ran, subtract $\frac{3}{5}$ (Carl's distance) from $\frac{5}{5}$ (the total distance) to get $\frac{2}{5}$. Then, multiply this fraction by the distance of the race. Multiply numerators ($2 \times 9 = 18$) to find the numerator and multiply denominators ($5 \times 10 = 50$) to find the denominator. Reduce the fraction $\frac{18}{50}$ to $\frac{9}{25}$.
3	B	To multiply a whole number by a mixed number, first change the whole number to a fraction ($\frac{3}{1}$) and change the mixed number to a fraction ($\frac{9}{5}$). Multiply numerators ($3 \times 9 = 27$) to find the numerator and multiply denominators ($1 \times 5 = 5$) to find the denominator. The improper fraction $\frac{27}{5}$ can be changed to the mixed number $5\frac{2}{5}$
4	C	To multiply a fraction by a mixed number, change the mixed number to a fraction ($\frac{16}{5}$). Multiply numerators ($2 \times 16 = 32$) to find the numerator and multiply denominators ($3 \times 5 = 15$) to find the denominator. The improper fraction $\frac{32}{15}$ can be changed to the mixed number $2\frac{2}{15}$.
5	B	To multiply a mixed number by a mixed number, change each mixed number to a fraction ($\frac{41}{2}$ and $\frac{9}{2}$). Multiply numerators ($41 \times 9 = 369$) to find the numerator and multiply denominators ($2 \times 2 = 4$) to find the denominator. The improper fraction $\frac{369}{4}$ can be changed to the mixed number $92\frac{1}{4}$.

Question No.	Answer	Detailed Explanations
6	A	To multiply a whole number by a mixed number, first change the whole number to a fraction $(\frac{20}{1})$ and change the mixed number to a fraction $(\frac{14}{3})$. Multiply numerators (20 x 14 = 280) to find the numerator and multiply denominators (1 x 3 = 3) to find the denominator. The improper fraction $\frac{280}{3}$ can be changed to the mixed number $93\frac{1}{3}$.
7	D	To multiply a whole number by a mixed number, first change the whole number to a fraction $(\frac{6}{1})$ and change the mixed number to a fraction $(\frac{9}{8})$. Multiply numerators (9 x 6 = 54) to find the numerator and multiply denominators (1 x 8 = 8) to find the denominator. The improper fraction $\frac{54}{8}$ can be changed to the mixed number $6\frac{6}{8}$.
8	D	To multiply a whole number by a mixed number, first change the whole number to a fraction $(\frac{21}{1})$ and change the mixed number to a fraction $(\frac{5}{4})$. Multiply numerators (21 x 5 = 105) to find the numerator and multiply denominators (1 x 4 = 4) to find the denominator. The improper fraction $\frac{105}{4}$ can be changed to the mixed number $26\frac{1}{4}$.
9	C	To change $\frac{14}{3}$ to a mixed number, divide 14 by 3. The number 4 remainder 2 is written as $4\frac{2}{3}$ because the remaining 2 still needs to be divided by 3.
10	B	Each whole foot has $\frac{4}{4}$ and Danny needs 5 whole feet, so 5 x $\frac{4}{4}$ = $\frac{20}{4}$. He also needs $\frac{1}{4}$ more, so that's $\frac{21}{4}$ total. He will need 21 pieces that are $\frac{1}{4}$ foot long.

Question No.	Answer	Detailed Explanations
11	A,C & D	Find the area of each answer choice and compare it to 1 m² and 2 m². When multiplying fraction and mixed numbers, rewrite the mixed number as an improper fraction, multiply the numerators and put this result over the product of the denominators, then simplify.

A. $1\frac{2}{5} \times 1\frac{1}{6} = \frac{7}{5} \times \frac{7}{6} = \frac{49}{30} = 1\frac{19}{30}$ m² This is between 1 and 2 m² and is a correct choice.

B. $2\frac{3}{4} \times \frac{7}{8} = \frac{11}{4} \times \frac{7}{8} = \frac{77}{32} = 2\frac{13}{32}$ m² This is not between 1 and 2 m2 and is NOT a correct choice.

C. $\frac{6}{5} \times \frac{8}{9} = \frac{48}{45} = 1\frac{3}{45} = 1\frac{1}{15}$ m² This is between 1 and 2 m² and is a correct choice.

D. $\frac{3}{7} \times 2\frac{4}{5} = \frac{3}{7} \times \frac{14}{5} = \frac{42}{35} = 1\frac{7}{35} = 1\frac{1}{5}$ m² This is between 1 and 2 m² and is a correct choice.

Question No.	Answer	Detailed Explanations
12	4 miles	To find how far Riley ran, multiply 6 by $\frac{2}{3}$. When multiplying a whole number by a fraction rewrite the whole number as a fraction with a denominator of 1. Then multiply the numerators and denominators. Finally simplify the answer to a fraction in simplest form or a mixed number.

$$6 \times \frac{2}{3} = \frac{6}{1} \times \frac{2}{3} = \frac{12}{3} = 4$$

Question No.	Answer	Detailed Explanations
13	C	To determine the fraction of the book Leila read on Tuesday, multiply $\frac{1}{12}$ by $\frac{3}{4}$. When multiplying fractions, multiply the numerators together and put it over the product of the denominators. Then simplify the result.

Fraction of the book Leila read on

$$\text{Tuesday} = \frac{1}{12} \times \frac{3}{4} = \frac{(1 \times 3)}{(12 \times 4)} = \frac{3}{48}$$

$$\frac{3}{48} = \frac{\frac{3}{3}}{\frac{48}{3}} = \frac{1}{16}$$

Lesson 9: Dividing Fractions

Question No.	Answer	Detailed Explanations
1	D	The first step in dividing by a fraction is to find its reciprocal, which is the reverse of its numerator and denominator. The fraction $\frac{1}{3}$ becomes $\frac{3}{1}$, or the whole number 3. Then solve by multiplying. $2 \times 3 = 6$.
2	A	The first step in dividing by a fraction is to find its reciprocal, which is the reverse of its numerator and denominator.
3	D	The first step in dividing by a fraction is to find its reciprocal, which is the reverse of its numerator and denominator. The fraction $\frac{2}{3}$ becomes $\frac{3}{2}$. Then solve by multiplying (use $\frac{3}{1}$ for the whole number 3): $\frac{3}{1} \times \frac{3}{2} = \frac{9}{2} = 4\frac{1}{2}$
4	C	Dividing by a number less than one causes the original number to become larger. When dividing by a fraction less than 1, multiplying by its reciprocal will create a situation in which you multiply by a larger number and divide by a smaller number, therefore increasing the size.
5	D	To divide $\frac{1}{3}$ by 5, multiply $\frac{1}{3}$ by the reciprocal of 5, which is $\frac{1}{5}$. $\frac{1}{3} \times \frac{1}{5} = \frac{1}{15}$.
6	B	To divide $\frac{1}{8}$ by 4, multiply $\frac{1}{8}$ by the reciprocal of 4, which is $\frac{1}{4}$. $\frac{1}{8} \times \frac{1}{4} = \frac{1}{32}$
7	C	To solve, divide 10 by $\frac{1}{3}$, multiply 10 (or $\frac{10}{1}$) by the reciprocal of $\frac{1}{3}$, which is $\frac{3}{1}$. $\frac{10}{1} \times \frac{3}{1} = \frac{30}{1}$
8	C	When dividing two numbers (such as $12 \div 4 = 3$), the answer can be checked by multiplying ($3 \times 4 = 12$). This is true for fractions as well. To check $\frac{1}{6} \div 3 = \frac{1}{18}$, multiply: $\frac{1}{18} \times \frac{3}{1} = \frac{3}{18} = \frac{1}{6}$
9	A	A fraction divided by a whole number will become a smaller fraction. For example, $\frac{1}{2} \div 6 = \frac{1}{12}$.

Question No.	Answer	Detailed Explanations
10	B	To solve, divide 8 by $\frac{1}{4}$, multiply 8(or $\frac{8}{1}$) by the reciprocal of $\frac{1}{4}$, which is $\frac{4}{1}$. $\frac{8}{1} \times \frac{4}{1} = \frac{32}{1} = 32$
11	C	When dividing two numbers (such as $12 \div 4 = 3$), the answer can be checked by multiplying ($3 \times 4 = 12$). This is true for fractions as well. To check $10 \div \frac{1}{4} = 40$, multiply: $40 \times \frac{1}{4} = \frac{40}{4} = 10$

12

	True	False
$6 \div \frac{1}{3} > 16$	●	○
$\frac{1}{4} \div 3 =$	○	●
$12 \div \frac{1}{6} < 80$	●	○
$\frac{1}{5} \div 2 > 9$	○	●

To divide a number by a fraction, multiply the number by the reciprocal of the fraction.

A. $6 \div \frac{1}{3} = \frac{6}{1} \times \frac{3}{1} = \frac{18}{1} = 18$ Since $18>16$, $6 \div \frac{1}{3}>16$ is a true statement.

B. $\frac{1}{4} \div 3 = \frac{1}{4} \div \frac{3}{1} = \frac{1}{4} \times \frac{1}{3} = \frac{1}{12}$ Since $\frac{1}{12} \neq \frac{3}{12}$, $\frac{1}{4} \div 3 = \frac{3}{12}$ is a false statement.

C. $12 \div \frac{1}{6} = \frac{12}{1} \div \frac{1}{6} = \frac{12}{1} \times \frac{6}{1} = \frac{72}{1} = 72$ Since $72<80$, $12 \div \frac{1}{6}<80$ is a true statement.

D. $\frac{1}{5} \div 2 = \frac{1}{5} \div \frac{2}{1} = \frac{1}{5} \times \frac{1}{2} = \frac{1}{10}$ Since $\frac{1}{10}<9$, $\frac{1}{5} \div 2 >9$ is a false statement.

Question No.	Answer	Detailed Explanations
13		When trying to find a divisor or dividend when working with fractions, rewrite the question as a multiplication question and then take the reciprocal of the second fraction.

A. $2 \times 6 = 12 \rightarrow 2 \div \frac{1}{6} = 12$

B. $3 \times 5 = 15 \rightarrow \frac{1}{3} \div 5 = \frac{1}{15}$

C. $12 \times 4 = 48 \rightarrow 12 \div \frac{1}{4} = 48$

D. $7 \times 4 = 28 \rightarrow \frac{1}{7} \div 4 = \frac{1}{28}$

Lesson 10: Dividing by Unit Fractions

Question No.	Answer	Detailed Explanations
1	B	Division can be checked by multiplying the quotient by the divisor to equal the dividend. In this case, $24 \times \frac{1}{4} = \frac{24}{4} = 6$.
2	D	In option D, each of four units is divided into thirds, resulting in a total of 12 units. Option B also produces 12 units, but it shows 3 units divided into fourths.
3	D	The model shows each of three units divided into eighths, resulting in a total of 24 units. That is shown as $3 \div \frac{1}{8} = 24$. Although option C is a true statement, it does not represent the model.
4	A	To solve, divide the 5 pieces of wood into fifths: $5 \div \frac{1}{5} = 5 \times 5 = 25$
5	C	To solve, divide the 10 yards of fabric into thirds: $10 \div \frac{1}{3} = 10 \times 3 = 30$
6	B	When dividing a whole number by a fraction, rewrite the whole number as a fraction with a denominator of 1. Then multiply by the multiplicative inverse of the fraction. Finally, simplify the answer. $4 \div \frac{1}{5} = \frac{4}{1} \times \frac{5}{1} = \frac{20}{1} = 20$. B is the right answer choice.

7

Statements	True	False
$\dfrac{1}{12} \div 4 > 40$		✓
$\dfrac{1}{4} \div 7 = \dfrac{1}{14}$		✓
$\dfrac{1}{3} \div 33 < 5$	✓	
$\dfrac{1}{8} \div 4 < \dfrac{1}{2}$	✓	

1) $\dfrac{1}{12} \div \dfrac{4}{1} = \dfrac{1}{12} \times \dfrac{1}{4} = \dfrac{1}{48}$; Therefore $\dfrac{1}{48} < 40$.

2) $\dfrac{1}{4} \div 7 = \dfrac{1}{4} \div \dfrac{7}{1} = \dfrac{1}{4} \times \dfrac{1}{7} = \dfrac{1}{28}$; Therefore $\dfrac{1}{28} \neq \dfrac{1}{14}$

3) $\dfrac{1}{3} \div 33 = \dfrac{1}{3} \div \dfrac{33}{1} = \dfrac{1}{3} \times \dfrac{1}{33} = \dfrac{1}{99}$; Therefore $\dfrac{1}{99} < 5$

4) $\dfrac{1}{8} \div 4 = \dfrac{1}{8} \div \dfrac{4}{1} = \dfrac{1}{8} \times \dfrac{1}{4} = \dfrac{1}{32}$; Therefore $\dfrac{1}{32} < \dfrac{1}{2}$

8

When trying to find a divisor when working with fractions quotients, rewrite the question as a multiplication question.

A. $\dfrac{1}{8} \times \dfrac{1}{14} = \dfrac{1}{112} \rightarrow \dfrac{1}{8} \div 14 = \dfrac{1}{112}$

B. $\dfrac{1}{3} \times \dfrac{1}{29} = \dfrac{1}{87} \rightarrow \dfrac{1}{3} \div 29 = \dfrac{1}{87}$

C. $\dfrac{1}{9} \times \dfrac{1}{55} = \dfrac{1}{495} \rightarrow \dfrac{1}{9} \div 55 = \dfrac{1}{495}$

9   A

$8 \div \dfrac{1}{3} = 8 \times 3 = 24$. The answer choice A is the correct answer.

10   B

$4 \div \dfrac{7}{21} = 4 \times \dfrac{21}{7}$

$= 4 \times 3$
$= 12$
B is the correct answer choice.

Lesson 11: Real World Problems Dividing Fractions

Question No.	Answer	Detailed Explanations
1	B	In option B, each of 3 units is divided into fourths, resulting in a total of 12 units. Option D also produces 12 units, but it shows 4 units divided into thirds.
2	A	The model shows each of 4 units divided into eighths, resulting in a total of 32 units. That shows how many $\frac{1}{8}$ units there are in the 4 whole units.
3	D	Divide $\frac{1}{4}$ mile by 3 to solve: $$\frac{1}{4} \div 3 =$$ $$\frac{1}{4} \times \frac{1}{3} = \frac{1}{12}$$
4	A	Divide $\frac{1}{10}$ liter by 6 to solve: $$\frac{1}{10} \div 6 =$$ $$\frac{1}{10} \times \frac{1}{6} = \frac{1}{60}$$
5	C	To solve, divide the 3 pizzas by $\frac{1}{12}$: $$3 \div \frac{1}{12} =$$ $$3 \times 12 = 36$$

Question No.	Answer	Detailed Explanations
6	A & C	To determine the number of silly putty portions each boy has, divided the number of packages into the respective portions given in the question. Then compare the number of portions. Lawson has five packages divided into thirds. This is $5 \div \frac{1}{3}$

$$5 \div \frac{1}{3} = \frac{5}{1} \div \frac{1}{3} = \frac{5}{1} \times \frac{1}{3} = 15 \text{ portions}$$

Rhett has four packages divided into fourths. This is represented by $4 \div \frac{1}{4}$

$$4 \div \frac{1}{4} = \frac{4}{1} \div \frac{1}{4} = \frac{4}{1} \times \frac{4}{1} = 16 \text{ portions}$$

Wynn has three packages divided into fifths. This is represented by $3 \div \frac{1}{5}$

$$3 \div \frac{1}{5} = \frac{3}{1} \div \frac{1}{5} = \frac{3}{1} \times \frac{5}{1} = 15 \text{ portions}$$

A. Both Lawson and Wynn have 16 portions. Statement A is true.
B. Wynn has one less portion than Rhett. Statement B is false.
C. Rhett has one more portion of sill putty than Lawson. Statement C is true.
D. All three boys do not have the same number of portions. Statement D is false.
The correct answer choices are A and C.

| 7 | $5\frac{1}{4}$ | To determine the maximum length, divide 6 by $1\frac{1}{7}$. |

$$6 \div 1\frac{1}{7} = 6 \div \frac{8}{7} = \frac{6}{1} \times \frac{7}{8} = \frac{42}{8} = 5\frac{2}{8} = 5\frac{1}{4}$$

Maximum length of the garden is $5\frac{1}{4}$ yards.

| 8 | B | There are 1000 milliliters in 1 liter. |

$$\frac{2500 \text{ ml}}{1} \times \frac{1 \text{ liter}}{1000 \text{ ml}} = \frac{2500}{1000} = 2.5 \text{ liters}$$

Answer Choice B is correct.

| 9 | A | $\frac{1}{2} \times 4 = 2$. |

Hence, 4 liters are required to paint all the rooms. The correct answer is A.

| 10 | B | Since, Mathew needs $\frac{1}{10}$ tank of fuel and has $\frac{4}{5}$ tank of fuel, we need to divide $\frac{4}{5}$ by $\frac{1}{10}$ |

$$\frac{4}{5} \times \frac{1}{10} = 8 \text{ days}$$ which is the correct answer. Hence, correct choice is B.

Chapter 5:
Measurement and Data

Lesson 1: Converting Units of Measure

You can scan the QR code given below or use the url to access additional EdSearch resources including videos and mobile apps related to *Converting Units of Measure*.

Converting Units of Measure

URL	QR Code
http://www.lumoslearning.com/a/5mda1	

1. Complete the following.
   1 inch equals the same length as _____ centimeters.

   Ⓐ 0.6
   Ⓑ 2.54
   Ⓒ 10
   Ⓓ 2.0

2. Complete the following.
   10 cm = 1 ___

   Ⓐ km
   Ⓑ dm
   Ⓒ mm
   Ⓓ m

3. Keith has 7 yards of string. How many inches of string does he have?

   Ⓐ 112 inches
   Ⓑ 224 inches
   Ⓒ 84 inches
   Ⓓ 252 inches

4. Which of these is the most reasonable estimate for the total area of the floor space in a house?

   Ⓐ 1,200 sq km
   Ⓑ 1,200 sq in
   Ⓒ 120 sq in
   Ⓓ 1,200 sq ft

5. Complete the following.
   2.25 hours = _____ minutes

   Ⓐ 135
   Ⓑ 225
   Ⓒ 145
   Ⓓ 150

6. The normal body temperature of a person in degrees Celsius is about _____ .

   Ⓐ 0 degrees Celsius
   Ⓑ 37 degrees Celsius
   Ⓒ 95 degrees Celsius
   Ⓓ 12 degrees Celsius

7. There are 8 pints in a gallon. How many times greater is the volume of a gallon compared to a pint?

   Ⓐ 8 times greater
   Ⓑ $\frac{1}{8}$ times greater
   Ⓒ twice as great
   Ⓓ $\frac{8}{10}$ as great

8. Which of the following measures about 1 dm in length?

   Ⓐ a car
   Ⓑ a new crayon
   Ⓒ a ladybug
   Ⓓ a football field

9. Complete the following.
   The area of a postage stamp is about _____ .

   Ⓐ 100 sq in
   Ⓑ 4 sq in
   Ⓒ 10 sq in
   Ⓓ 1 sq in

10. Complete the following.
    A fully loaded moving truck might weigh _____ .

    Ⓐ 5 tons
    Ⓑ 50 tons
    Ⓒ 500 ounces
    Ⓓ 5,000 ounces

11. Read the conversions and indicate whether they are true or false.

	True	False
45 quarts = 90 cups	○	○
15 liters = 15,000 milliliters	○	○
5 pounds = 80 ounces	○	○
60 inches = 5 feet	○	○

12. A meter is 100 centimeters. If a track is 500 meters long. How long is the track in centimeters? Enter your answer in the box given below.

13. Complete the following statement:
75 nickels has the same value as _____ quarters.

14. Kale made 5 gallons of sports drink for the baseball team. Which of the following represents the same quantity? Select all the correct answers.

Ⓐ 20 quarts
Ⓑ 32 pints
Ⓒ 40 cups
Ⓓ 640 ounces

Chapter 5

Lesson 2: Representing and Interpreting Data

You can scan the QR code given below or use the url to access additional EdSearch resources including videos and mobile apps related to *Representing and Interpreting Data.*

 ## Representing and Interpreting Data

URL	QR Code
http://www.lumoslearning.com/a/5mdb2	

1. **A 5th grade science class is raising mealworms. The students measured the mealworms and recorded the lengths on this line plot.**

Length of Mealworms

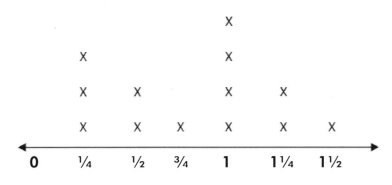

Inches

According to this line plot, what was the length of the longest mealworm?

Ⓐ $\frac{1}{4}$ inch

Ⓑ $\frac{3}{4}$ inch

Ⓒ 1 inch

Ⓓ $1\frac{1}{2}$ inches

2. **A 5th grade science class is raising mealworms. The students measured the mealworms and recorded the lengths on this line plot.**

Length of Mealworms

```
                            X
            X               X
            X       X       X       X
            X       X   X   X   X   X
◄───────────────────────────────────────►
     0     ¼     ½    ¾    1    1¼    1½
```

Inches

According to this line plot, what was the length of the shortest mealworm?

Ⓐ $\frac{1}{4}$ inch

Ⓑ $\frac{3}{4}$ inch

Ⓒ $1\frac{1}{4}$ inch

Ⓓ 0

3. **A 5th grade science class is raising mealworms. The students measured the mealworms and recorded the lengths on this line plot.**

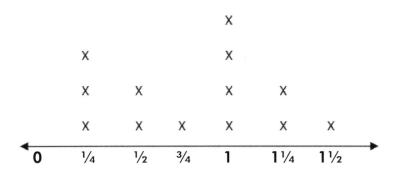

According to this line plot, what was the most common length for mealworms?

Ⓐ $1\frac{1}{2}$ inches

Ⓑ $\frac{3}{4}$ inch

Ⓒ $\frac{1}{4}$ inch

Ⓓ 1 inch

4. **A 5th grade science class is raising mealworms. The students measured the mealworms and recorded the lengths on this line plot.**

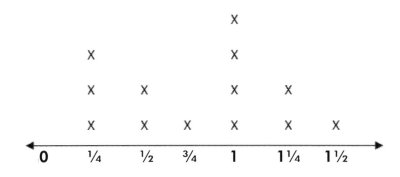

According to this line plot, how many mealworms were less than 1 inch long?

Ⓐ 4

Ⓑ 6

Ⓒ 3

Ⓓ 2

5. **A 5th grade science class is raising mealworms. The students measured the mealworms and recorded the lengths on this line plot.**

Length of Mealworms

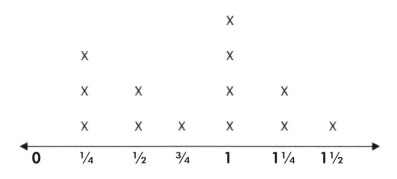

According to this line plot, how many mealworms were measured in all?

Ⓐ 4
Ⓑ 10
Ⓒ 13
Ⓓ $27\frac{3}{4}$

6. **A 5th grade science class is raising mealworms. The students measured the mealworms and recorded the lengths on this line plot.**

Length of Mealworms

```
                    X
      X             X
      X     X       X     X
      X     X   X   X   X   X
 ◄────┼─────┼───┼───┼───┼───┼───────►
  0   ¼    ½   ¾   1  1¼  1½
```

Inches

According to this line plot, what is the median length of a mealworm?

Ⓐ 1 inch
Ⓑ 13 inches

Ⓒ between $\frac{3}{4}$ inch and 1 inch

Ⓓ $1\frac{1}{2}$ inches

7. **A 5th grade science class is raising mealworms. The students measured the mealworms and recorded the lengths on this line plot.**

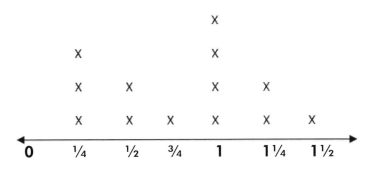

Length of Mealworms

Inches

How could someone use this line plot to find the total length of all the mealworms?

Ⓐ Add each of the numbers along the bottom of the line plot
Ⓑ Multiply each of the numbers along the bottom of the line plot
Ⓒ Multiply each length by its number of Xs, then add the values
Ⓓ Multiply each of the numbers along the bottom of the line plot by the total number of Xs, then add the values

8. **A 5th grade science class is raising mealworms. The students measured the mealworms and recorded the lengths on this line plot.**

Length of Mealworms

Inches

Which of these mealworm lengths would not fit within the range of this line plot?

Ⓐ $\frac{7}{8}$ inch

Ⓑ $1\frac{3}{4}$ inches

Ⓒ $1\frac{1}{8}$ inches

Ⓓ $\frac{5}{16}$ inch

9. **A 5th grade science class is observing weather conditions. The students measured the amount of precipitation each day and recorded it on this line plot.**

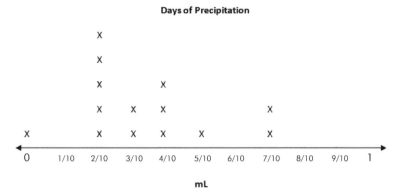

According to this line plot, what was the most precipitation recorded in one day?

Ⓐ $4\frac{7}{10}$ mL

Ⓑ $\frac{7}{10}$ mL

Ⓒ $\frac{9}{10}$ mL

Ⓓ $\frac{2}{10}$ mL

10. **A 5th grade science class is observing weather conditions. The students measured the amount of precipitation each day and recorded it on this line plot.**

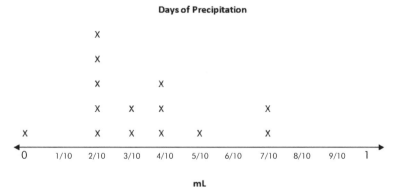

According to this line plot, what was the least amount of precipitation that fell on days that had precipitation?

Ⓐ $\frac{1}{10}$ mL

Ⓑ $\frac{6}{10}$ mL

Ⓒ 0 mL

Ⓓ $\frac{2}{10}$ mL

11. A 5th grade science class is observing weather conditions. The students measured the amount of precipitation each day and recorded it on this line plot.

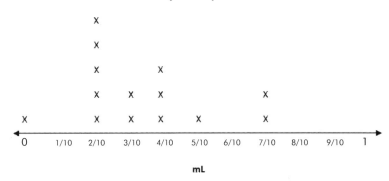

According to this line plot, what was the most common amount of precipitation?

Ⓐ $\frac{7}{10}$ mL

Ⓑ $\frac{9}{10}$ mL

Ⓒ $\frac{2}{10}$ mL

Ⓓ 0 mL

12. A 5th grade science class is observing weather conditions. The students measured the amount of precipitation each day and recorded it on this line plot.

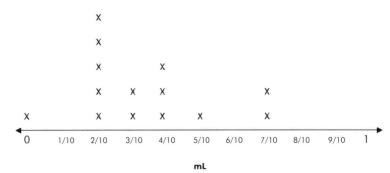

According to this line plot, how many days received less than $\frac{3}{10}$ mL of precipitation?

Ⓐ 6
Ⓑ 0
Ⓒ 4
Ⓓ 3

13. A 5th grade science class is observing weather conditions. The students measured the amount of precipitation each day and recorded it on this line plot.

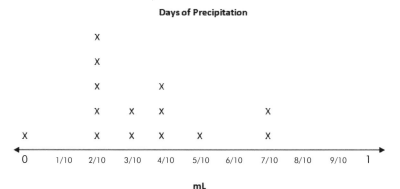

According to this line plot, how many days were observed in all?

Ⓐ 13
Ⓑ 5
Ⓒ 14
Ⓓ 11

14. A 5th grade science class is observing weather conditions. The students measured the amount of precipitation each day and recorded it on this line plot.

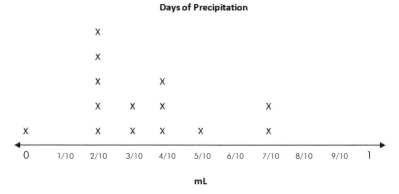

According to this line plot, what is the median amount of precipitation?

Ⓐ $\frac{7}{10}$ mL
Ⓑ $\frac{3}{10}$ mL
Ⓒ $\frac{2}{10}$ mL
Ⓓ 0 mL

15. **A 5th grade science class is observing weather conditions. The students measured the amount of precipitation each day and recorded it on this line plot.**

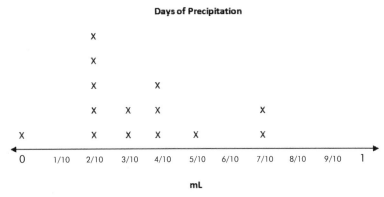

How could someone use this line plot to find the total amount of all the precipitation that fell?

Ⓐ Add each of the numbers along the bottom of the line plot
Ⓑ Multiply each of the numbers along the bottom of the line plot by the total number of Xs, then add the values
Ⓒ Multiply each of the numbers along the bottom of the line plot
Ⓓ Multiply each measurement by its number of Xs, then add the values

16. **A 5th grade science class is observing weather conditions. The students measured the amount of precipitation each day and recorded it on this line plot.**

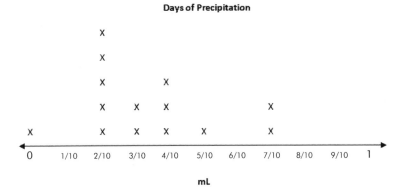

Which of these measurements would not fit within the range of this line plot?

Ⓐ $\frac{12}{10}$ mL
Ⓑ $\frac{9}{10}$ mL
Ⓒ 0 mL
Ⓓ $\frac{2}{10}$ mL

17. **A 5th grade science class is observing weather conditions. The students measured the amount of precipitation each day and recorded it on this line plot.**

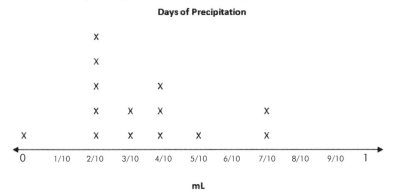

Suppose the class recorded data for one more day, but there was no precipitation. What should they do?

Ⓐ Leave the line plot as it is
Ⓑ Add an X above the one in the 0 column
Ⓒ Erase one of the Xs from the line plot
Ⓓ Make up a value and put an X in that column

18. **A 5th grade science class went on a nature walk. Each of the students selected one leaf and weighed it when they got back to the room. They recorded their data on this line plot.**

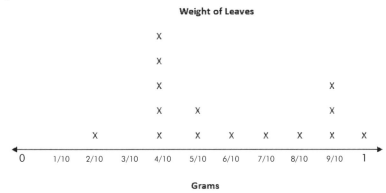

According to this line plot, which is the least frequent weight of a leaf from the choices given below?

Ⓐ $\frac{7}{10}$ g
Ⓑ $\frac{9}{10}$ g
Ⓒ $\frac{4}{10}$ g
Ⓓ $\frac{5}{10}$ g

19. **A 5th grade science class went on a nature walk. Each of the students selected one leaf and weighed it when they got back to the room. They recorded their data on this line plot.**

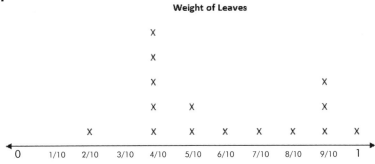

According to this line plot, what is the range of weights for these leaves?

Ⓐ $\frac{8}{10}$ g

Ⓑ 1 g

Ⓒ $\frac{5}{10}$ g

Ⓓ $\frac{4}{10}$ g

20. **A 5th grade science class went on a nature walk. Each of the students selected one leaf and weighed it when they got back to the room. They recorded their data on this line plot.**

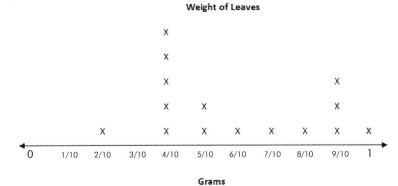

According to this line plot, what is the mode for this set of data?

Ⓐ 1
Ⓑ 15
Ⓒ $\frac{5}{10}$
Ⓓ $\frac{4}{10}$

21. A 5th grade science class went on a nature walk. Each of the students selected one leaf and weighed it when they got back to the room. They recorded their data on this line plot.

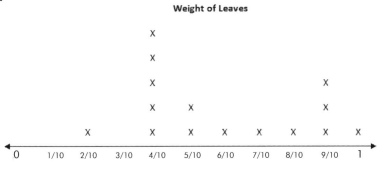

According to this line plot, how many leaves weigh more than $\frac{7}{10}$ g?

Ⓐ 1
Ⓑ 5
Ⓒ 9
Ⓓ 0

22. A 5th grade science class went on a nature walk. Each of the students selected one leaf and weighed it when they got back to the room. They recorded their data on this line plot.

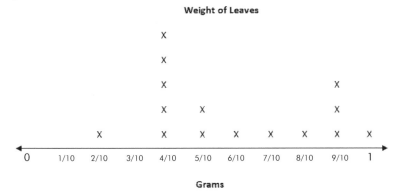

According to this line plot, how many leaves were measured in all?

Ⓐ 15
Ⓑ $\frac{4}{10}$
Ⓒ $\frac{6}{10}$
Ⓓ 11

23. **A 5th grade science class went on a nature walk. Each of the students selected one leaf and weighed it when they got back to the room. They recorded their data on this line plot.**

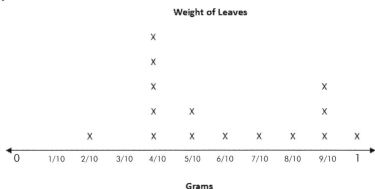

According to this line plot, how many leaves weigh less than the most frequent weight?

Ⓐ 9
Ⓑ 5
Ⓒ 0
Ⓓ 1

24. **A 5th grade science class went on a nature walk. Each of the students selected one leaf and weighed it when they got back to the room. They recorded their data on this line plot.**

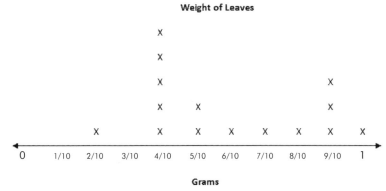

What is the total weight of all the leaves?

Ⓐ 9 g
Ⓑ $\frac{9}{10}$ g
Ⓒ 90 g
Ⓓ $\frac{9}{100}$ g

25. A 5th grade science class went on a nature walk. Each of the students selected one leaf and weighed it when they got back to the room. They recorded their data on this line plot.

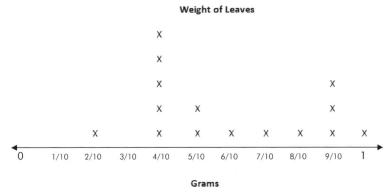

Weight of Leaves

Grams

What is the average weight of the leaves?

Ⓐ $\frac{5}{10}$ g

Ⓑ $\frac{9}{10}$ g

Ⓒ $\frac{6}{10}$ g

Ⓓ $\frac{8}{10}$ g

26. The line plot below shows the weight in fractions of a gram for fifteen pieces of mail. How much does each of the 3 pieces of mails next to 1/2 gram weigh?

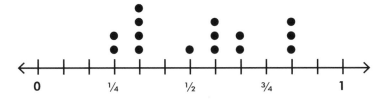

27. The line plot below shows the length in fractions of an inch of several pieces of tile all having the same width. If the pieces were lined up length to length, how long would the line of tiles be? Circle the correct answer.

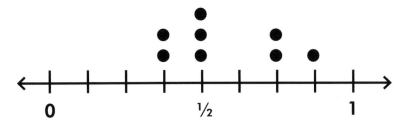

Ⓐ $3\dfrac{1}{4}$

Ⓑ $3\dfrac{5}{8}$

Ⓒ $1\dfrac{4}{8}$

Ⓓ $4\dfrac{5}{8}$

28. Tabitha made a line plot of the following data

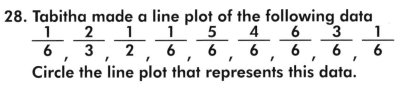

Circle the line plot that represents this data.

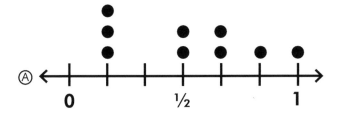

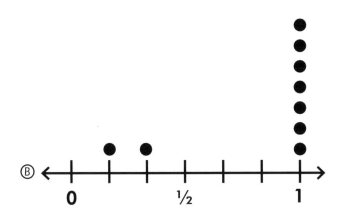

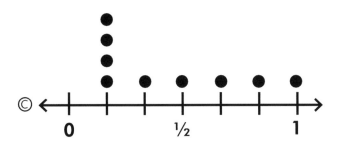

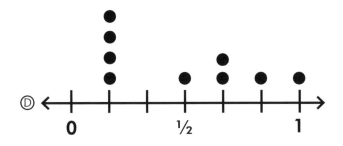

Chapter 5

Lesson 3: Volume

You can scan the QR code given below or use the url to access additional EdSearch resources including videos and mobile apps related to *Volume*.

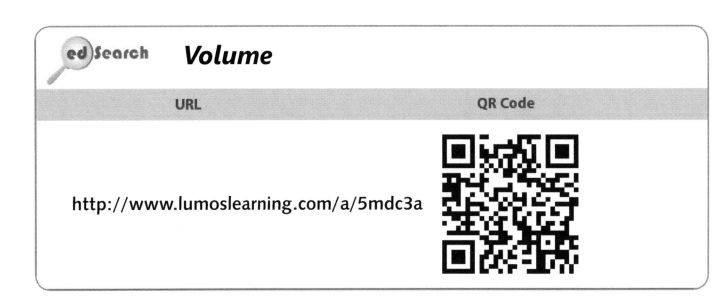

ed)Search	Volume	
URL		QR Code
http://www.lumoslearning.com/a/5mdc3a		

1. Which type of unit might be used to record the volume of a rectangular prism?

   Ⓐ inches
   Ⓑ square inches
   Ⓒ ounces
   Ⓓ cubic inches

2. Maeve needed to pack a crate that measured 4 ft. by 2 ft. by 3 ft. with 1 foot cubes. How many 1 foot cubes can she fit in the crate?

   Ⓐ 12
   Ⓑ 48
   Ⓒ 24
   Ⓓ 9

3. The volume of an object is the amount of _____.

   Ⓐ space it occupies
   Ⓑ dimensions it has
   Ⓒ layers you can put in it
   Ⓓ weight it can hold

4. Which of these could be filled with about 160 cubes of sugar if each sugar cube is one cubic centimeter?

   Ⓐ a ring box
   Ⓑ a moving box
   Ⓒ a cereal box
   Ⓓ a sandbox

5. Tony and Yolani are measuring the volume of a supply box at school. Tony uses a ruler to measure the box's length, width, and height in centimeters; then he multiplies these measurements. Yolani fills the box with centimeter cubes, then counts the number of cubes. How will their answers compare?

   Ⓐ They cannot be compared because they used different units.
   Ⓑ They will be almost or exactly the same.
   Ⓒ Tony's answer will be greater than Yolani's.
   Ⓓ Yolani's answer will be greater than Tony's.

6. **Complete the following:**
   A cereal box has a volume of about _____ .

   Ⓐ 3.0 cubic inches
   Ⓑ 3,000 cubic inches
   Ⓒ 30 cubic inches
   Ⓓ 300 cubic inches

7. **Complete the following:**
   The correct formula for finding the volume of a rectangular box with length l, width w, and height h is _____ .

   Ⓐ $V = l \times w \times h$
   Ⓑ $V = l \times w + h$
   Ⓒ $V = w \times h + l$
   Ⓓ $V = l + w + h$

8. **What is the volume of a box that measures 36 in. by 24 in. by 24 in.?**

   Ⓐ 20,763 cubic inches
   Ⓑ 84 cubic inches
   Ⓒ 20,736 cubic inches
   Ⓓ 111 cubic inches

9. **What is the volume of a box that measures 8 by 3 by 12 inches?**

   Ⓐ 882 cubic inches
   Ⓑ 23 cubic inches
   Ⓒ 280 cubic inches
   Ⓓ 288 cubic inches

10. **What is the volume of a cube that measures 3 by 3 by 3 centimeters?**

    Ⓐ 9 cubic cm
    Ⓑ 12 cubic cm
    Ⓒ 27 cubic cm
    Ⓓ 6 cubic cm

11. Which of the following cubes is a unit cube? Select Yes or No.

	YES	NO
3 cm, 4 cm, 1 cm cube	○	○
1 in, 1 in, 1 in cube	○	○
6 m, 6 m, 6 m cube	○	○
1 unit, 1 unit cube	○	○

12. Oscar wants to determine the volume of the chest, shown in the picture, in cubic inches. Complete the sentence below describing the dimensions of the unit cube.

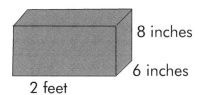

8 inches

6 inches

2 feet

Unit cube length	
Unit cube width	
Unit cube height	

13. Isaiah needs to determine the volume of his locker as shown in the picture. Which of the following unit cubes can he use to find the volume? Select the two correct answers.

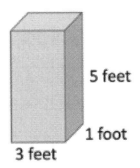

5 feet

1 foot

3 feet

Ⓐ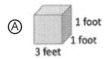

1 foot
1 foot
3 feet

Ⓑ

1 in
1 in
1 in

Ⓒ

5 feet
1 foot
3 feet

Ⓓ

1 foot
1 foot
1 foot

Chapter 5

Lesson 4: Cubic Units

You can scan the QR code given below or use the url to access additional EdSearch resources including videos and mobile apps related to *Cubic Units*.

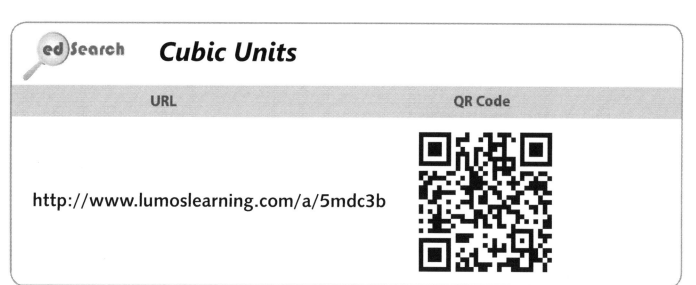

ed)Search   *Cubic Units*

URL	QR Code
http://www.lumoslearning.com/a/5mdc3b	

1. **Stan covers the bottom of a box of 8 centimeters by 8 centimeters with unit cubes, leaving no gaps. He is able to build 4 layers of cubes to fill the box completely. What is the volume of the box?**

   Ⓐ 256 centimeters
   Ⓑ The square of 256 cm
   Ⓒ 256 cm^2
   Ⓓ 256 cubic centimeters

2. **Which of these is an accurate way to measure the volume of a rectangular prism?**

   Ⓐ Fill it with water and then weigh the water
   Ⓑ Trace each face of the prism on centimeter grid paper, and then count the number of squares it comprises
   Ⓒ Measure the length and the width, and then multiply the two values
   Ⓓ Pack it with unit cubes, leaving no gaps or overlaps, and count the number of unit cubes

3. **Which of these could possibly be the volume of a cereal box?**

   Ⓐ 360 in^3
   Ⓑ 520 sq cm
   Ⓒ 400 cubic feet
   Ⓓ 385 dm^2

4. **A container measures 4 inches wide, 6 inches long, and 10 inches high. How many 1 inch cubes will it hold?**

   Ⓐ 20^2
   Ⓑ 240
   Ⓒ The cube of 240
   Ⓓ Cannot be determined

5. **Annie covers the bottom of a box with 6 centimeter cubes (A centimeter cube is a cube of dimensions 1 cm x 1 cm x 1 cm), leaving no gaps. If the volume of the box is 30 cm^3, how many more centimeter cubes will she be able to fit inside?**

   Ⓐ 5
   Ⓑ 180
   Ⓒ 24
   Ⓓ 4

6. The rectangular prism shown has 4 layers and each layer has 12 cubes. If one cube is equal to 1 cubic centimeter, what is the volume of the prism? Enter your answer in the box given below.

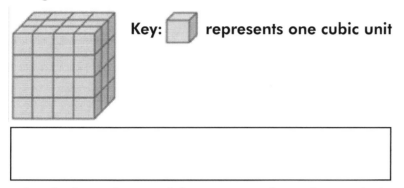

Key: represents one cubic unit

| |
| |

7. What is the volume of the rectangular prism? Circle the correct answer choice.

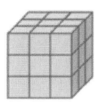

Key: represents one cubic unit

Ⓐ 27 cubic units
Ⓑ 18 cubic units
Ⓒ 16 cubic units
Ⓓ 21 cubic units

8. Select the picture that has a volume of 12 cubic units.

Key: represents one cubic unit

Ⓐ

Ⓑ

Ⓒ

Ⓓ

9. **What is the volume of this figure?**

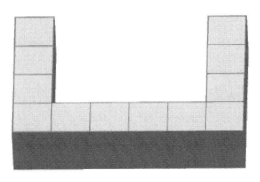

Key: represents one cubic unit

Ⓐ 12
Ⓑ 16
Ⓒ 18
Ⓓ 20

10. **What is the volume of this figure?**

Key: represents one cubic unit

Ⓐ 6
Ⓑ 8
Ⓒ 9
Ⓓ 10

Chapter 5

Lesson 5: Counting Cubic Units

You can scan the QR code given below or use the url to access additional EdSearch resources including videos and mobile apps related to *Counting Cubic Units*.

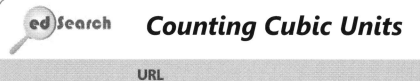

URL	QR Code
http://www.lumoslearning.com/a/5mdc4	

1. **What is the volume of the figure?**

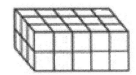

Ⓐ 60 cubic units
Ⓑ 15 cubic units
Ⓒ 30 cubic units
Ⓓ 31 cubic units

2. **What is the volume of the figure?**

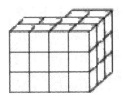

Ⓐ 30 units^3
Ⓑ 27 units^3
Ⓒ 31 units^3
Ⓓ 36 units^3

3. **Which of these has a volume of 24 cubic units?**

Ⓐ

Ⓑ

Ⓒ

Ⓓ

4. Trevor is building a tower out of centimeter cubes. This is the base of the tower so far.

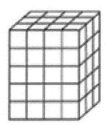

How many more layers must Trevor add to have a tower with a volume of 84 cm³?

Ⓐ 7
Ⓑ 2
Ⓒ 5
Ⓓ 4

5. Kerry built the figure on the left and Milo built the one on the right. If they knock down their two figures to build one large one using all of the blocks, what will its volume be?

 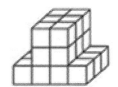

Ⓐ 34 cubic units
Ⓑ 16 cubic units
Ⓒ 52 cubic units
Ⓓ 40 cubic units

6. Garrett must build a building that has a volume of 11 cubic meters. Look at the buildings below and indicate which are possible designs for his building.
Volume of one cube is one cubic meter.

	Yes	No
	○	○
	○	○
	○	○
	○	○

7. Use the picture of the solid below to complete the table. Write the numbers (only) in the blank spaces provided.

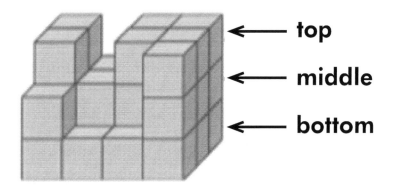

Number of cubes in the bottom layer	
Number of cubes in the middle layer	
Number of cubes in the top layer	
Volume of the solid	

Chapter 5

Lesson 6: Multiply to Find Volume

You can scan the QR code given below or use the url to access additional EdSearch resources including videos and mobile apps related to *Multiply to Find Volume*.

 **Multiply to Find Volume**

URL	QR Code
http://www.lumoslearning.com/a/5mdc5a	

1. **What is the volume of the figure?**

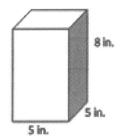

8 in.

5 in.

5 in.

Ⓐ 33 in³
Ⓑ 18 in³
Ⓒ 80 in³
Ⓓ 200 in³

2. **What is the volume of the figure?**

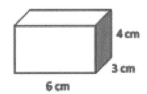

4 cm

3 cm

6 cm

Ⓐ 13 cm³
Ⓑ 22 cm³
Ⓒ 72 cm³
Ⓓ 700 cm³

3. **The figure has a volume of 66 ft³. What is the height of the figure?**

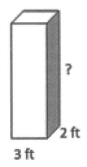

?

2 ft

3 ft

Ⓐ 11 ft
Ⓑ 61 ft
Ⓒ 13 ft
Ⓓ 33 ft

4. The figure has a volume of 14 in³. What is the width of the figure?

2 in.

?

7 in.

Ⓐ 2 inches
Ⓑ 1 inch
Ⓒ 5 inches
Ⓓ 2.5 inches

5. Which figure has a volume of 42 m³?

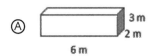

Ⓐ

3 m
2 m
6 m

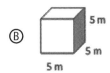

Ⓑ

5 m
5 m
5 m

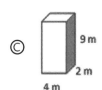

Ⓒ

9 m
2 m
4 m

Ⓓ

2 m
3 m
7 m

6. Use the picture to answer the question.

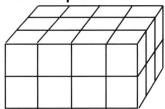

Which of the following will result in the volume of the figure. Note that more than one option may be correct.

Ⓐ 3 X 4 X 2
Ⓑ (4 X 3) + 2
Ⓒ 8 X 3
Ⓓ 12 + 2

7. Piko filled a box with 4 layers of cubes that measured one foot on each side. If the bottom of the box fits 6 cubes, What is the volume of the box? Enter the answer in the box.

8. Sarah is making a rectangular prism with base as shown below.

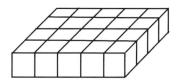

She plans to have a height of 5 cubes. Find the volume of the rectangular prism.

Ⓐ 110 cubic units
Ⓑ 100 cubic units
Ⓒ 125 cubic units
Ⓓ 135 cubic units

9. Find the volume of the rectangular prism given below.
   Note: The volume of 1 cube is equal to one cubic unit.

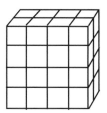

Ⓐ 32 cubic units
Ⓑ 36 cubic units
Ⓒ 48 cubic units
Ⓓ 54 cubic units

10. The base of a rectangular prism has an area of 25 square units. The height of the rectangular prism is 2 units. What is the volume of the prism?

Ⓐ 50 cubic units
Ⓑ 100 cubic units
Ⓒ 75 cubic units
Ⓓ 125 cubic units

Lesson 7: Real World Problems with Volume

You can scan the QR code given below or use the url to access additional EdSearch resources including videos and mobile apps related to *Real World Problems with Volume*.

 **Real World Problems with Volume**

URL	QR Code
http://www.lumoslearning.com/a/5mdc5b	

1. Michael packed a box full of 1 ft cubes. The box held 54 cubes. Which of these could be the box Michael packed?

    Ⓐ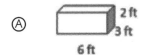
    2 ft
    3 ft
    6 ft

    Ⓑ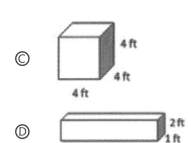
    9 ft
    2 ft
    3 ft

    Ⓒ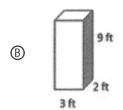
    4 ft
    4 ft
    4 ft

    Ⓓ
    2 ft
    1 ft
    18 ft

2. A container is shaped like a rectangular prism. The area of its base is 30 in². If the container is 5 inches tall, how many 1 inch cubes can it hold?

    Ⓐ 150
    Ⓑ 35
    Ⓒ 4500
    Ⓓ 95

3. A rectangular prism has a volume of 300 cm³. If the area of its base is 25 cm² how tall is the prism?

    Ⓐ 325 cm
    Ⓑ 7500 cm
    Ⓒ 12 cm
    Ⓓ 275 cm

4. Antonia wants to buy a jewelry box with the greatest volume. She measures the length, width, and height of four different jewelry boxes. Which one should she buy to have the greatest volume?

    Ⓐ 10 in x 7 in x 4 in
    Ⓑ 8 in x 5 in x 5 in
    Ⓒ 12 in x 5 in x 5 in
    Ⓓ 14 in x 2 in x 10 in

5. Damien is building a file cabinet that must hold 20 ft³. He has created a base for the cabinet that is 4 ft by 1 ft. How tall should he build the cabinet?

Ⓐ 25 ft
Ⓑ 20 ft
Ⓒ 4 ft
Ⓓ 5 ft

6. Bethany has a small rectangular garden that is 32 inches long by 14 inches wide. The average depth of the soil is 2 inches. If Bethany wanted to replace the soil, how much would she need? Circle the correct answer choice.

Ⓐ 448 in³
Ⓑ 896 in³
Ⓒ 450 in³
Ⓓ 48 in³

7. A building has a volume of 1520 ft³. The area of the base of the building is 95 ft². What is the height of the building?

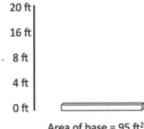

Area of base = 95 ft²

Ⓐ 20ft
Ⓑ 16ft
Ⓒ 8ft
Ⓓ 4ft

8. Melanie has a jewelry box with the volume of 36 cubic cms. If the width is 4 cms and the height is 3 cms, then what is the length of the box?

Ⓐ 4 cms
Ⓑ 3 cms
Ⓒ 5 cms
Ⓓ 12 cms

9. Henry is building an aquarium. The length of the aquarium is 4 feet, width is 3 feet and the height is 5 feet. What will be the volume of the aquarium?

Ⓐ 64 cubic feet
Ⓑ 72 cubic feet
Ⓒ 60 cubic feet
Ⓓ 81 cubic feet.

10. Volume of a clothes box is 2m x 1m x 2m. 15 such boxes must be loaded in a tanker. What will be the total volume occupied by the boxes?

Ⓐ 72 cubic meters
Ⓑ 64 cubic meters
Ⓒ 81 cubic meters
Ⓓ 60 cubic meters

Chapter 5

Lesson 8: Adding Volumes

You can scan the QR code given below or use the url to access additional EdSearch resources including videos and mobile apps related to *Adding Volumes*.

ed)Search **Adding Volumes**

URL	QR Code
http://www.lumoslearning.com/a/5mdc5c	

1. A refrigerator has a 3 foot by 2 foot base. The refrigerator portion is 4 feet high and the freezer is 2 feet high. What is the total volume?

Ⓐ 36 ft³
Ⓑ 26 ft³
Ⓒ 11 ft³
Ⓓ 16 ft³

2. Matthew has two identical coolers. Each one measures 30 inches long, 10 inches wide, and 15 inches high. What is the total volume of the two coolers?

Ⓐ 4,500 in³
Ⓑ 9,000 in³
Ⓒ 110 in³
Ⓓ 3,025 in³

3. Ingrid is packing 1 foot square boxes into shipping crates. She has two shipping crates, shown below. How many boxes can she pack in them all together?

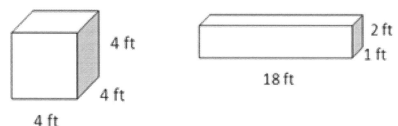

Ⓐ 64
Ⓑ 33
Ⓒ 82
Ⓓ 100

4. Bryson has two identical bookcases stacked one on top of the other. Together, they hold 48 ft³. If the area of the base is 8 ft², how tall is each bookcase?

Ⓐ 40 ft
Ⓑ 6 ft
Ⓒ 3 ft
Ⓓ 20 ft

5. Amy built a house for her gerbil out of two boxes. One box measures 6 cm by 3 cm by 10 cm and the other measures 4 cm by 2 cm by 2 cm. What is the total volume of the gerbil house?

Ⓐ 196 cm³
Ⓑ 180 cm³
Ⓒ 27 cm³
Ⓓ 2,880 cm³

6. Jade and her brother Seth are going on a hiking trip. Together they can bring a total of 345 in³ of supplies. Indicate by checking yes or no the possible dimensions of the box each can bring.

	Yes	No
Jade: 4 in X 12 in X4 in Seth: 8 in X 7 in X 3 in	○	○
Jade: 8 in X 5 in X 5 in Seth: 4 in X 11 in X 3 in	○	○
Jade: 3 in X 9 in X 6 in Seth: 8 in X 13 in X 1 in	○	○
Jade: 6 in X 13 in X 4 in Seth: 3 in X 8 in X 2 in	○	○

7. A three-section warehouse holds a total of 24,766 ft³ of volume. The first section has a storage area of 436 ft² and a height of 19 ft. The second section has a height of 15 ft. and a depth of 26 ft. The volume of the first two sections is 17,254 ft³. Based on this information, complete the table below.

Volume of first section in cubic feet	
Length of the second section in feet	
Volume of the third section in cubic feet	

End of Measurement and Data

Chapter 5:

Measurement and Data

Answer Key
&
Detailed Explanations

Lesson 1: Converting Units of Measure

Question No.	Answer	Detailed Explanations
1	B	An inch is a larger unit of measure than a centimeter, so the correct answer must be more than one. There are actually 2.54 centimeters to an inch.
2	B	The prefix deci means ten. One dm (decimeter) is 10 centimeters in length.
3	D	There are 12 inches in a foot and 3 feet in a yard. Therefore, each yard is made up of 36 inches (3 x 12 = 36). Seven yards would be 7 x 36 inches, which is 252.
4	D	Square inches are relatively small units of measure. Even 1,200 of them would be smaller than the area of one room. Square kilometers are relatively large units of measure. Even one sq km would be larger than a house. The only reasonable answer is 1,200 sq ft.
5	A	There are 60 minutes in each hour, so multiply: $\begin{array}{r} 2.25 \\ \times\ 60 \\ \hline 000 \\ 13500 \\ \hline 135.00 \end{array}$
6	B	At 0 degrees Celsius, water freezes. At 100 degrees Celsius, water boils. The only reasonable temperature for a human body is somewhere in between. The best estimate is 37 degrees Celsius.
7	A	8 pints =1 gallon, a gallon is 8 times greater in volume than a pint.
8	B	The prefix deci means ten. One dm (decimeter) is 10 centimeters in length. Option B is the correct answer. A crayon measures approximately 10 cms or 1 dm. Car and football field are very big and hence, options A and D are not correct. A Ladybug approximately measures 1 cm and hence, Option C is also incorrect.
9	D	The area of an object is equal to its length x width. A postage stamp is about 1 in long and 1 in wide, so its area is about 1 sq in. The other answer options would all be much larger than a postage stamp.
10	A	Ounces are unreasonable estimates for this scenario, even if there are 5,000 of them (that's about 300 pounds). Loaded trucks are measured in tons, with one ton equal to 2,000 pounds. Five tons is equal to 10,000 pounds (5 x 2,000), which is a reasonable estimate for a loaded truck. The option 50 tons (50 x 2,000) is equal to 100,000 pounds, which is much too large.

LumosLearning.com

Question No.	Answer	Detailed Explanations

11

	True	False
45 quarts = 90 cups	○	●
15 liters = 15,000 milliliters	●	○
5 pounds = 80 ounces	●	○
60 inches = 5 feet	●	○

$$\frac{45 \text{ quarts}}{1} \times \frac{2 \text{ pints}}{1 \text{ quart}} \times \frac{2 \text{ cups}}{1 \text{ pint}} = 180 \text{ cups}$$

$$\frac{15 \text{ liters}}{1} \times \frac{1000 \text{ ml}}{1 \text{ liter}} = 15000 \text{ ml}$$

$$\frac{5 \text{ Pounds}}{1} \times \frac{16 \text{ ounces}}{1 \text{ pound}} = 80 \text{ ounces}$$

$$\frac{60 \text{ Inches}}{1} \times \frac{1 \text{ foot}}{12 \text{ Inches}} = \frac{60}{12} = 5 \text{ feet}$$

12 — **50,000 cm** — If 1 meter is 100 centimeters then there are 100 centimeters in one meter. So if the track is 500 meters long it is 500 x 100 = 50,000 centimeters long.

13 — **15** — The value of 75 nickels is 75 x $0.05 = $3.75. To find the number of quarters, divide $3.75 by 0.25 to get an answer of 15.
Another way to think of this problem is that a nickel is worth one fifth of a quarter. One fifth of 75 (75 ÷ 5) is 15.

14 — **A & D** —
A. There are 4 quarts in 1 gallon.
$$\frac{5 \text{ gallons}}{1} \times \frac{4 \text{ quarts}}{1 \text{ gallon}} = \frac{20 \text{ quarts}}{1 \text{ pint}} = 20 \text{ quarts}$$

B. There are 2 pints in 1 quart or 8 pints in 1 gallon.
$$\frac{5 \text{ gallons}}{1} \times \frac{8 \text{ pints}}{1 \text{ gallon}} = \frac{40 \text{ pints}}{1} = 40 \text{ pints}$$

C. There are 2 cups in 1 pint or 16 cups in 1 gallon.
$$\frac{5 \text{ gallons}}{1} \times \frac{16 \text{ cups}}{1 \text{ gallon}} = \frac{80 \text{ cups}}{1} = 80 \text{ cups}$$

D. There are 8 ounces in 1 cup or 128 ounces in 1 gallon.
$$\frac{5 \text{ gallons}}{1} \times \frac{128 \text{ ounces}}{1 \text{ gallon}} = \frac{640 \text{ ounces}}{1} = 640 \text{ ounces}$$

Lesson 2: Representing and Interpreting Data

Question No.	Answer	Detailed Explanations
1	D	The length of each mealworm is shown along the bottom of the line plot. The highest value on the scale is $1\frac{1}{2}$ inches and the Xs above show that there were mealworms this long.
2	A	The length of each mealworm is shown along the bottom of the line plot. The lowest value on the scale is $\frac{1}{4}$ inch and the Xs above show that there were mealworms this long.
3	D	The Xs on the line plot represent the number of mealworms at each length. Since 1 inch has the most Xs above it (4), it is the most common length.
4	B	The Xs on the line plot represent the number of mealworms at each length. There were 3 mealworms that were $\frac{1}{4}$ inch long, 2 that were $\frac{1}{2}$ inch long, and 1 that was $\frac{3}{4}$ inch long. Altogether, that's 6 mealworms that are less than 1 inch long.
5	C	The Xs on the line plot represent the number of mealworms at each length. There are 13 Xs in all, at various lengths.
6	C	**Rule:** If the number data are odd, there will be one middle number which will be the median. If the number of data are even, there will be two middle numbers and the average of these numbers gives the median of the data set. The median value would be between $\frac{3}{4}$ inch and 1 inch because the number of data is 6.
7	C	To find the total length, you would have to add together the three mealworms that are $\frac{1}{4}$ inch long ($3 \times \frac{1}{4}$) plus the two that are $\frac{1}{2}$ inch long ($2 \times \frac{1}{2}$) and so on for each length.
8	B	$1\frac{3}{4}$ inches is greater than $1\frac{1}{2}$ inches, so it would not fall within the range of $\frac{1}{4}$ to $1\frac{1}{2}$ inches as all of the other measurements.
9	B	The amount of precipitation each day is shown along the bottom of the line plot. The highest value on the scale that has Xs above it, showing that there was a day that received that amount, is $\frac{7}{10}$ mL.
10	D	The amount of precipitation each day is shown along the bottom of the line plot. The lowest value on the scale other than zero that has Xs above it is $\frac{2}{10}$ mL.

Question No.	Answer	Detailed Explanations
11	C	The Xs on the line plot represent the number of days that received that much precipitation. Since $\frac{2}{10}$ mL has the most Xs above it (5 Xs), it is the most common amount.
12	A	The Xs on the line plot represent the number of days that received that amount of precipitation. There was 1 day that received 0 mL and 5 days that received $\frac{2}{10}$ mL. Altogether, that's 6 days that received less than $\frac{3}{10}$ mL of precipitation.
13	C	The Xs on the line plot represent the number of days that received a certain amount of precipitation. There are 14 Xs in all, at various amounts.
14	B	The median of a set of data is the middle value. In this set of 14 data points, the middle value would be one of the $\frac{3}{10}$ mL recordings.
15	D	To find the total amount, you would have to add together the 5 days that received $\frac{2}{10}$ mL ($5 \times \frac{2}{10}$) plus the 2 that received $\frac{3}{10}$ mL ($2 \times \frac{3}{10}$) and so on for each data point.
16	A	$\frac{12}{10}$ mL is greater than 1 mL, so it would not fall within the range of 0 to 1 mL as all of the other measurements do.
17	B	All measurements need to be recorded. If there was 0 precipitation on that day, students should mark an X above the one in the 0 column.
18	A	The value $\frac{7}{10}$ g has only one X above it, which means only one leaf weighed this much. The other values given have more than one X above them, indicating that more than one leaf had that weight. This makes $\frac{7}{10}$ the least frequent of these options.
19	A	The range for a set of data is the difference between the highest and lowest data points. On this line plot, the highest value is 1 and the lowest value is $\frac{2}{10}$, so the range is $\frac{8}{10}$.
20	D	The mode for a set of data is the value that occurs most frequently. Since $\frac{4}{10}$ g has the most Xs above it 5 total, it is the most frequent weight.

Question No.	Answer	Detailed Explanations
21	B	The Xs on the line plot represent the number of leaves at each weight. There is one leaf that weighs $\frac{8}{10}$ g, three that weigh $\frac{9}{10}$ g, and one that weighs 1 g. Altogether, that's 5 leaves that weigh more than $\frac{7}{10}$ g.
22	A	The Xs on the line plot represent the number of leaves at each weight. There are 15 Xs in all, at various weights.
23	D	The most frequent weight for this set of data is $\frac{4}{10}$ g, which has 5 data points. The only leaf that weighs less than these is the one leaf that weighs $\frac{2}{10}$ g.
24	A	To find the total weight, you would have to add together the weight of the one leaf that is $\frac{2}{10}$ g $(1 \times \frac{2}{10})$ plus the five that are $\frac{4}{10}$ g $(5 \times \frac{4}{10})$ and so on for each data point. The total will be $\frac{90}{10}$ g, which is equal to 9 g.
25	C	To find the average weight of the leaves, multiply the number of leaves with their respective weights and add them to get 9 grams. Divide this by the total number of leaves (15) to get $\frac{6}{10}$ grams.$$\frac{2}{10} + (\frac{4}{10} \times 5) + (\frac{5}{10} \times 2) + \frac{6}{10} + \frac{7}{10} + \frac{8}{10} + (\frac{9}{10} \times 3) + \frac{10}{10}$$ To find the average, we need to divide by 15 $$= \frac{\frac{2}{10} + \frac{20}{10} + \frac{10}{10} + \frac{6}{10} + \frac{7}{10} + \frac{8}{10} + \frac{27}{10} + \frac{10}{10}}{15}$$ $$= \frac{\frac{90}{10}}{15}$$ $$= \frac{3}{5} = 0.6 \text{ grams or } \frac{6}{10} \text{ grams.}$$

Question No.	Answer	Detailed Explanations
26	$\frac{7}{12}$	There are twelve divisions between 0 and 1. Thus distance between two successive divisions represents $\frac{1}{12}$ of a gram. Therefore the seventh division line represents $\frac{7}{12}$. There are three dots above this division to represent three pieces of mail. Therefore the correct answer is $\frac{7}{12}$.
27	D	Number line between 0 and 1 is divided into 8 equal segments. Therefore, the markings refer to $\frac{1}{8}$, $\frac{2}{8}$ etc. First two dots represent two tiles of lengths $\frac{3}{8}$ of an inch. Next three dots represent three tiles of lengths $\frac{4}{8}$ of an inch (Though $\frac{4}{8} = \frac{1}{2}$, it is better to keep the first fraction with denominator 8; it will be easier to add the fractions). Next two tiles have lengths of $\frac{6}{8}$ of an inch and the last one has a length of $\frac{7}{8}$ of an inch. Therefore, total length of the line of tiles (L) is given by, $L = (2 \times \frac{3}{8}) + (3 \times \frac{4}{8}) + (2 \times \frac{6}{8}) + (1 \times \frac{7}{8})$ $L = \frac{6}{8} + \frac{12}{8} + \frac{12}{8} + \frac{7}{8} = \frac{(6+12+12+7)}{8} = \frac{37}{8} = 4\frac{5}{8}$ inches Therefore the correct answer is D.
28	A	Since there are six division between 0 and 1, each division is $\frac{1}{6}$ convert each fraction that does not have a denominator of 6, to an equivalent fraction with a denominator of 6. The list of data points becomes $\frac{1}{6}, \frac{4}{6}, \frac{3}{6}, \frac{1}{6}, \frac{5}{6}, \frac{4}{6}, \frac{6}{6}, \frac{3}{6}, \frac{1}{6}$ Then order the fractions: $\frac{1}{6}, \frac{1}{6}, \frac{1}{6}, \frac{3}{6}, \frac{3}{6}, \frac{4}{6}, \frac{4}{6}, \frac{5}{6}, \frac{6}{6}$ then place a dot above each division for each fraction representing that division.

Lesson 3: Volume

Question No.	Answer	Detailed Explanations
1	D	To find the volume of a rectangular solid, multiply the area of the base (l x w) by the height (h). Therefore, the units are cubic units of length, such as cubic inches.
2	C	To find the volume of a rectangular solid, multiply the area of the base (l x w) by the height (h). In this problem, 4 x 2 x 3 = 24 cubic feet. Therefore, it will take 24 cubes to fill the crate, since each cube is one cubic foot.
3	A	Volume is a measurement of the space an object occupies. It is measured in cubic units.
4	C	The formula for determining volume is l x w x h. A cereal box could be about 8 cm x 2 cm x 10 cm, which is 160 cm³.
5	B	The formula for determining volume is l x w x h. It can also be determined by counting the number of unit cubes that fill a solid figure. Since Tony and Yolani both used centimeters as their units, their two methods should give them almost the same answer.
6	D	One cubic inch is roughly the size of a die. The best estimate for the number of cubic inches it would take to fill a regular cereal box is about 300. The actual volume of a cereal box can be found by multiplying its length x width x height, so an estimate of 10 x 2 x 15 inches is reasonable.
7	A	To find the volume of a rectangular solid multiply the area of the base (l x w) by the height (h).
8	C	To find the volume of a solid multiply the area of the base (l x w) by the height (h). In this problem, 36 x 24 x 24 = 20,736 cubic inches.
9	D	To find the volume of a solid multiply the area of the base (l x w) by the height (h). In this problem, 8 x 3 x 12 = 288 cubic inches.
10	C	To find the volume of a solid multiply the area of the base (l x w) by the height (h). In this problem, 3 x 3 x 3 = 27 cubic centimeters.

Question No.	Answer	Detailed Explanations

11

	YES	NO
3 cm 4 cm 1 cm	○	●
1 in 1 in 1 in	●	○
6 m 6 m 6 m	○	●
1 unit 1 unit	○	●

A unit cube is a cube that has a length, width and depth of one unit. The unit can be anything such as meters, inches, feet.
A. This is not a unit cube because not all dimensions are 1 cm.
B. This is a unit cube because all dimensions are 1 inch.
C. This is not a unit cube because all three dimensions are not 1 m.
D. This is a unit square, not a unit cube.

12 — **1,1,1**

Unit cube length	1
Unit cube width	1
Unit cube height	1

Because Oscar wants to determine the volume in cubic inches he should use a cube that represents a cubic inch. Such a cube would be 1 inch by 1 inch by 1 inch.

13 — **B &D**

1 in x 1 in x 1 in and 1 foot x 1 foot x 1 foot are unit cubes. Though other two cubes (3 feet x 1 foot x 1 foot and 3 feet x 1 foot x 5 feet) also can be used to measure the volume of the locker, they are not unit cubes. Hence the correct answers are options (B) and (D).

Lesson 4: Cubic Units

Question No.	Answer	Detailed Explanations
1	D	The volume of a container is measured in cubic units (or units^3).
2	D	An object's volume can be determined by packing it with unit cubes, leaving no gaps or overlaps, and counting the number of unit cubes.
3	A	This is the best option because not only is the value reasonable (a cereal box could measure 3 in × 10 in × 12 in, for example), but it also uses units appropriate for measuring volume.
4	B	The volume of the container is 240 in^3 (4 x 6 x 10). That means it can hold 240 1-inch cubes.
5	C	If the volume of the box is 30 cm^3, it can hold 30 centimeter cubes. Since there are already 6 in the box, there is room for 24 more (30 − 6 = 24).
6	48	To determine the volume or total number of cubes, multiply the number of cubes in each layer by the number of layers. 12 × 4 = 48 cubic cm.
7	A	To determine the volume of the rectangular prism, count the number of cubes. Each layer has 9 cubes and there are three layers so 9 × 3 = 27 cubes. The volume of the prism is 27 cubic units, choice A.
8	B	Count the number of cubes. The picture with 12 cubes has a volume of 12 cubic units. The first picture has 16 cubes, the second 12, the third 8 and the fourth 16.
9	A	Count each of the squares as 1 cube, we get total of 12, hence, the correct answer choice is 12.
10	A	Count each of the squares as 1 cube, we get total of 6, hence, the correct answer choice is 6.

Lesson 5: Counting Cubic Units

Question No.	Answer	Detailed Explanations
1	C	The figure clearly has 15 cubes in the top layer, so there must be another 15 cubes in the bottom layer (the figure is only 2 units high, or 2 layers). Therefore, it has a volume of 30 cubic units (15 + 15 = 30).
2	A	By counting the number of cubes in the figure, you can find that the volume is 30 units^3. There are 3 layers of 8 cubes each in the front part of the figure (3 x 8 = 24) and 3 layers of 2 cubes each at the back of the figure (3 x 2 = 6). Therefore, 24 + 6 = 30.
3	D	By counting the number of cubes in the figure, you can find that the volume is 24 units^3. The bottom layer is 4 by 3 units, so it has a volume of 12 units^3. Each of the top 2 layers is 2 by 3 units, so they each have a volume of 6 units^3. Therefore, 12 + 6 + 6 = 24 units^3.
4	B	The base of the tower measures 4 x 3 x 5, which gives it a volume of 60 cm^3. Since each layer is 4 x 3, it has a volume of 12 cm^3. In order to reach 84 cm^3, Trevor must add 2 more layers (2 × 12 = 24 and 24 + 60 = 84).
5	D	Kerry's figure has a volume of 16 cubic units (you can see 8 cubes at the front of the figure and there are another 8 behind). Trevor's figure has a volume of 24 cubic units (The bottom layer is 4 by 3 units, so it has a volume of 12 units^3. Each of the top 2 layers is 2 by 3 units, so they each have a volume of 6 units^3. Therefore, the volume of Milo's figure is 12 + 6 + 6 = 24 units^3.) Together, their tower's volume is 40 cubic units (16 + 24 = 40).

Question No.	Answer	Detailed Explanations

6 — Garrett's building must have exactly 11 cubes. Count the cubes in each design. If the design has 11 cubes answer yes. If not answer is no.

First and fourth design have 12 cubes, Second one has 11 cubes, third one has 13 cubes.

	Yes	No
		•
	•	
		•
		•

7 — Number of cubes in the bottom layer 12
Number of cubes in the middle layer 10
Number of cubes in the top layer 7
The volume of the solid is the sum of the cubes, which is 29.

Lesson 6: Multiply to Find Volume

Question No.	Answer	Detailed Explanations
1	D	To find the volume of a rectangular prism, multiply the length × width × height (5 × 5 × 8 = 200).
2	C	To find the volume of a rectangular prism, multiply the length × width × height (6 × 3 × 4 = 72).
3	A	Since the volume (66 ft³) must equal length × width × height, then 2 × 3 × 11 = 66.
4	B	Since the volume (14 in³) must equal length × width × height, then 7 × 1 × 2 = 14.
5	D	To find the volume of a rectangular prism, multiply the length × width × height (7 x 3 x 2 = 42).
6	A & C	The volume of the figure is equal to the number of cubes that will fit in the box. This can be determined by multiplying the number of cubes on each side, 3 × 4 × 2 = 24. Another way is to find how many cubes are in the bottom layer and multiply by the number of layers, (3 × 4) × 2 = 12 × 2 = 24. A third way is to find the number of cubes in the front and multiply that by the number of layers deep, (4 × 2) × 3 = 8 × 3 = 24. Therefore the correct answer choices are A and C.
7	24	The volume of the box is equal to the number of cubes that will fit in the box. If six cubes fit on the bottom and there were four layers, the number of cubes is 6 × 4 = 24. Since each cube was 1 foot on each side or volume = 1 cubic feet, the volume of the box is 24 cubic feet.
8	B	The base has 4 × 5 cubes and height of 5 cubes. Hence, the volume is 4 × 5 × 5 = 100 cubic units. Hence, the correct answer choice is B.
9	A	The base has 4 × 2 cubes and height of 4 cubes. Hence, the volume is 4 × 2 × 4 = 32 cubic units. Hence, the correct answer choice is A.
10	A	The volume is 25 × 2 = 50 cubic units. Hence, correct answer choice is A.

Lesson 7: Real World Problems with Volume

Question No.	Answer	Detailed Explanations
1	B	A box that holds 54 one feet cubes has a volume of 54 ft³. To find the box with this volume, multiply the length × width × height (3 × 2 × 9 = 54).
2	A	The number of 1 inch cubes it can hold is equal to its volume in inches³. To find the volume of the container, multiply the area of the base (30) by its height (5). 30 × 5 = 150.
3	C	The volume of the container (300 cm³) is equal to the area of the base (25) times its height. Therefore, 300 = 25 × 12.
4	C	To find the volume of a rectangular prism, multiply the length × width × height (12 × 5 × 5 = 300). This is greater than the other three jewelry boxes: 10 × 7 × 4 = 280 8 × 5 × 5 = 200 14 × 2 × 10 = 280
5	D	The volume of the cabinet (20 ft³) will be equal to the area of the base (4 × 1 = 4) times its height. Therefore, the height should be 5 ft (20 = 4 × 5).
6	B	To determine the amount of soil Bethany would need, find the volume of the garden. Volume = l × w × h = 32 × 14 × 2 = 896 in³.
7	B	To find the height of the building, use the formula, Volume(V)=Area of the (B) x height(h) V= Bh 1520 = 95h $h = \frac{1520}{95} = 16$ feet
8	B	Volume is given by l × 4 × 3 = 36 $L = \frac{36}{4 \times 3}$ Here, l = 3 cms. The correct answer is B.
9	C	Volume is given by = 4 × 3 × 5 = 60 cubic feet. Hence, the correct answer is C.
10	D	Volume occupied is given by 2 × 1 × 2 × 15 = 60 cubic meters. Hence, correct answer choice is D.

Lesson 8: Adding Volumes

Question No.	Answer	Detailed Explanations
1	A	To find the total volume, add the volume of the refrigerator ($2 \times 3 \times 4 = 24$) to the volume of the freezer ($2 \times 3 \times 2 = 12$). $24 + 12 = 36$
2	B	To find the volume of one cooler, multiply the length × width × height ($30 \times 10 \times 15 = 4,500$). Since Matthew has two coolers, add the two identical volumes: $4,500 + 4,500 = 9,000$
3	D	To find the total volume (the number of cubes she can pack), add the volume of the first crate ($4 \times 4 \times 4 = 64$) to the volume of the second crate ($18 \times 2 \times 1 = 36$). $64 + 36 = 100$
4	C	Since $V = b \times h$, the bookcases must be 6 ft tall together ($48 = 8 \times 6$). Therefore, each bookcase must be 3 ft tall ($3 + 3 = 6$).
5	A	To find the total volume, add the volume of the first box ($6 \times 3 \times 10 = 180$) to the volume of the second box ($4 \times 2 \times 2 = 16$). $180 + 16 = 196$
6		Find the volume of each box, and the volumes and the compare the sum to 345 in².

	Yes	No
Jade: 4 in × 12 in × 4 in = 192 in³ Seth: 8 in × 7 in × 3 in = 168 in³ 192 + 168 = 360 in³; 360>345		✓
Jade: 8 in × 5 in × 5 in = 200 in³ Seth: 4 in × 11 in × 3 in = 132 in³ 200 + 132 = 332 in³; 332<345	✓	
Jade: 3 in × 9 in × 6 in = 162 in³ Seth: 8 in × 13 in × 1 in = 104 in³ 162 + 104 = 266 in³; 266<345	✓	
Jade: 6 in × 13 in × 4 in = 312 in³ Seth: 3 in × 8 in × 2 in = 48 in³ 312 + 48 = 360 in³; 360>345		✓

Question No.	Answer	Detailed Explanations	
7		Volume of first section in cubic feet	**8284**
		Length of the second section in feet	**23**
		Volume of the third section in cubic feet	**7512**

(1) Volume of first section = Area of the base x height = 436 × 19 = 8284 cubic feet.

(2) To calculate the length of second section, first we have to calculate its volume.
Volume of the second section = Total volume of first and second section - volume of first section = 17254 - 8284 = 8970 cubic feet.
Volume = length × depth × height. Therefore, length = volume / (depth x height) = $\dfrac{8970}{26 \times 15}$ = $\dfrac{8970}{390}$ = 23 feet.

(3) Volume of third section = Total volume of the warehouse - (sum of volume of first and second section) = 24766 - 17254 = 7512 cubic feet.

Chapter 6:
Geometry

You can scan the QR code given below or use the url to access additional EdSearch resources including videos and mobile apps related to *Coordinate Geometry*.

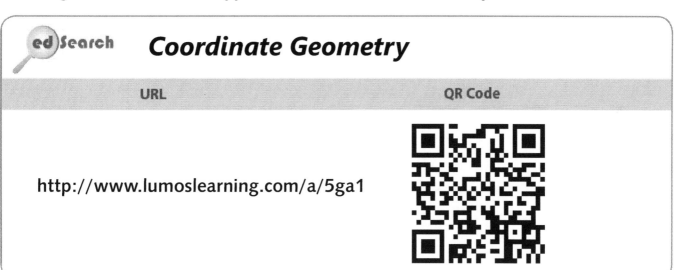

ed Search	**Coordinate Geometry**
URL	**QR Code**
http://www.lumoslearning.com/a/5ga1	

1. **Assume Point D was added to the grid so that Shape ABCD was a rectangle. Which of these could be the ordered pair for Point D?**

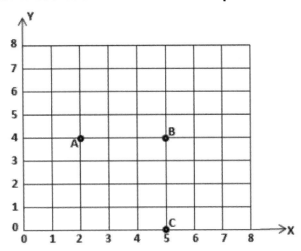

Ⓐ (0, 0)
Ⓑ (0, 2)
Ⓒ (2, 0)
Ⓓ (2, 2)

2. **Assume Segments AB and BC were drawn. Compare the lengths of the two segments.**

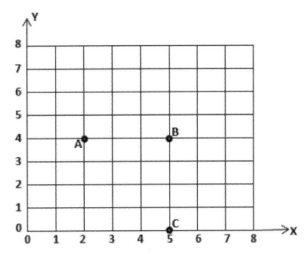

Ⓐ Segment AB is longer than Segment BC.
Ⓑ Segment BC is longer than Segment AB.
Ⓒ Segments AB and BC have the same length.
Ⓓ It cannot be determined from this information.

3.

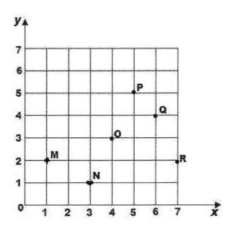

Where is Point R located?

Ⓐ (2, 7)
Ⓑ (7, 2)
Ⓒ (6, 4)
Ⓓ (4, 6)

4. Which point is located at (4, 3)?

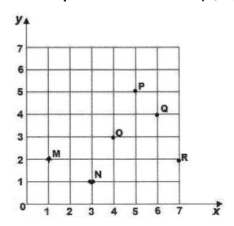

Ⓐ Point N
Ⓑ Point P
Ⓒ Point Q
Ⓓ Point O

5. Locate Point P on the coordinate grid. Which of the following ordered pairs represents its position?

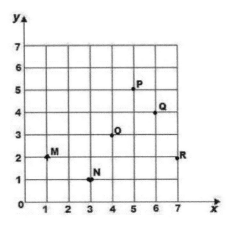

Ⓐ (5, 5)
Ⓑ (3, 1)
Ⓒ (1, 2)
Ⓓ (7, 2)

6. The graph below represents the values listed in the accompanying table, and their linear relationship. Use the graph and the table to respond to the following:
What is the value of c (in the table)?

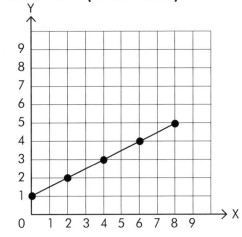

X	Y
0	1
4	a
2	b
8	5
c	4

Ⓐ c = 9
Ⓑ c = 7
Ⓒ c = 6
Ⓓ c = 5

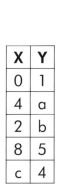

7. The graph below represents the values listed in the accompanying table, and their linear relationship. Use the graph and the table to respond to the following:
What is the value of b (in the table)?

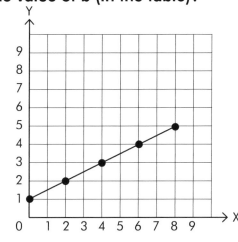

X	Y
0	1
4	a
2	b
8	5
c	4

Ⓐ b = 1
Ⓑ b = 2
Ⓒ b = 3
Ⓓ b = 6

8. Which of the following graphs best represents the values in this table?

x	y
1	1
2	2
3	3

Ⓐ

Ⓑ

Ⓒ

Ⓓ

9. **On a coordinate grid, which of these points would be closest to the origin?**

    Ⓐ (2, 1)
    Ⓑ (2, 7)
    Ⓒ (1, 5)
    Ⓓ (0, 4)

10. **If these four ordered pairs were plotted to form a diamond, which point would be the top of the diamond?**

    Ⓐ (2, 4)
    Ⓑ (5, 8)
    Ⓒ (8, 4)
    Ⓓ (5, 0)

11. **Points A (3, 2), B (6, 2), C (6, 6) and D (3, 7) are plotted on a coordinate grid. What type of polygon is ABCD?**

    Ⓐ a rectangle
    Ⓑ a rhombus
    Ⓒ a parallelogram
    Ⓓ a trapezoid

12. **The graph below represents the values listed in the accompanying table, and their linear relationship. Use the graph and the table to respond to the following:**
    Which of the following rules describes the behavior of this function?

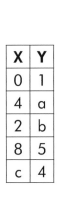

X	Y
0	1
4	a
2	b
8	5
c	4

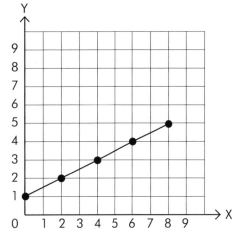

    Ⓐ y is equal to one more than x
    Ⓑ y is equal to twice x
    Ⓒ y is equal to one more than half of x
    Ⓓ y is equal to one more than twice x

13.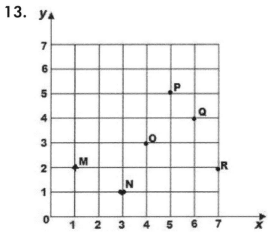

Assume points O, P, and Q form three vertices of a parallelogram. Which ordered pair could be the fourth vertex of that parallelogram?

Ⓐ (3, 3)
Ⓑ (4, 4)
Ⓒ (3, 5)
Ⓓ (3, 4)

14. Which of the following graphs best represents the values in this table?

x	y
3	1
3	2
3	3

Ⓐ

Ⓑ

Ⓒ

Ⓓ

15. If the functions x = y + 1 and y = 3 were plotted on a coordinate grid, which of these would be true?

Ⓐ They would intersect once.
Ⓑ They would form parallel lines.
Ⓒ They would intersect more than once.
Ⓓ They would form perpendicular lines.

16. Circle the letter that represents the x- axis.

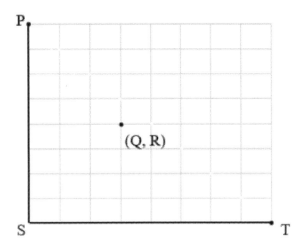

Ⓐ P
Ⓑ S
Ⓒ T

17. Which of the following are the coordinates of points A, B and C?
Circle the correct answer choice.

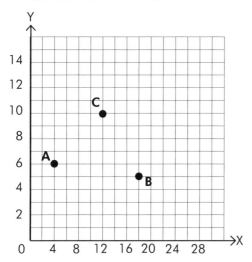

Ⓐ Point A: (2,6); Point B: (9,5); Point C: (6, 10)

Ⓑ Point A: (4,6); Point B: (12, 10); Point C: (18,5)

Ⓒ Point A: (4,6); Point B: (18, 5); Point C: (12,10)

Ⓓ Point A: (6,4); Point B: (10,12); Point C: (18,5)

Chapter 6

Lesson 2: Real World Graphing Problems

You can scan the QR code given below or use the url to access additional EdSearch resources including videos and mobile apps related to *Real World Graphing Problems*.

 *Real World Graphing Problems*

URL	QR Code
http://www.lumoslearning.com/a/5ga2	

1. According to the map, what is the location of the weather station (⚡)?

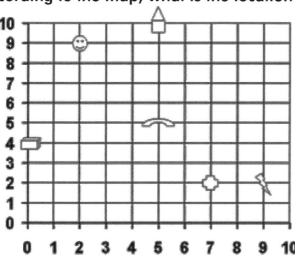

Ⓐ (3,9)
Ⓑ (8,2)
Ⓒ (9,2)
Ⓓ (2,9)

2. According to the map, what is the location of the warehouse (▱)?

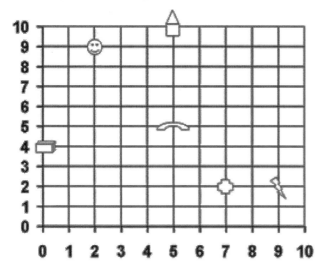

Ⓐ (x = 4)
Ⓑ (0,4)
Ⓒ (y = 4)
Ⓓ (4,0)

3. **According to the map, which is located at (7,2)?**

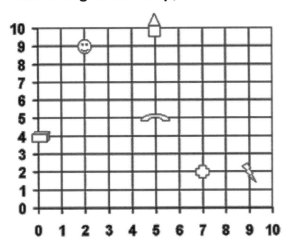

Ⓐ The hospital ⌗

Ⓑ The bridge ⌒

Ⓒ The playground ☺

Ⓓ The house ⌂

4. **According to the map, which is located at (5,5)?**

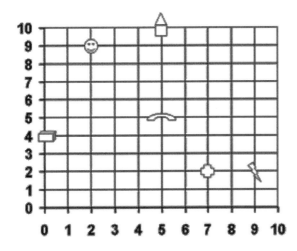

Ⓐ The hospital ⌗

Ⓑ The bridge ⌒

Ⓒ The playground ☺

Ⓓ The house ⌂

5. Which set of directions would lead a person from the playground (😊) to the hospital (⊞)?

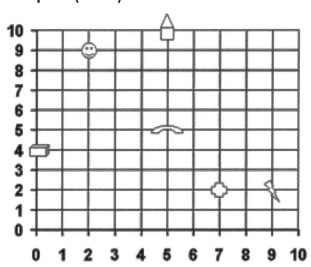

Ⓐ Walk 5 units along -ve y-axis and 7 units along +ve x-axis.
Ⓑ Walk 7 units along -ve y-axis and 2 units along +ve x-axis.
Ⓒ Walk 2 units along -ve y-axis and 7 units along +ve x-axis.
Ⓓ Walk 7 units along -ve y-axis and 5 units along +ve x-axis.

6. Which set of directions would lead a person from the weather station (⚡) to the bridge (⌒)?

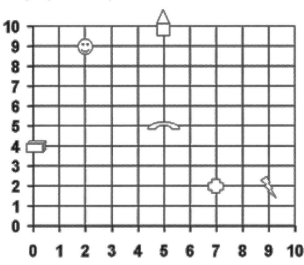

Ⓐ Walk 5 units along -ve x-axis and 5 units along +ve y-axis.
Ⓑ Walk 2 units along -ve x-axis and 0 units along +ve y-axis.
Ⓒ Walk 4 units along -ve x-axis and 3 units along +ve y-axis.
Ⓓ Walk 3 units along -ve x-axis and 4 units along +ve y-axis.

7. Where should the town locate a new lumber mill so it is as close as possible to both the warehouse ( ) and the hospital ( )?

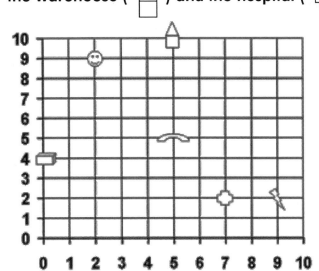

Ⓐ (7,0)
Ⓑ (5,3)
Ⓒ (1,7)
Ⓓ (5,0)

8. According to the map, what is the location of the zebras ( )?

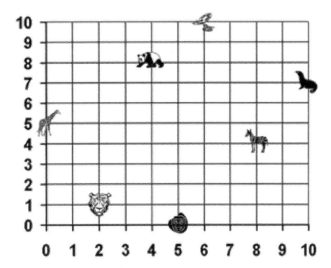

Ⓐ (8,4)
Ⓑ (8,0)
Ⓒ (4,8)
Ⓓ (4,4)

9. According to the map, what is the location of the giraffes ( )?

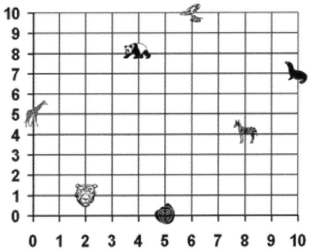

Ⓐ (y = 5)
Ⓑ (0,5)
Ⓒ (x = 5)
Ⓓ (5,0)

10. According to the map, which is located at (10,7)?

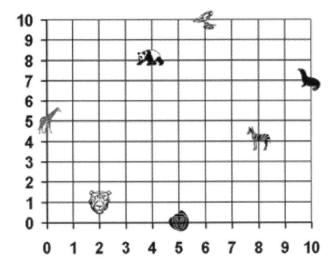

Ⓐ The tigers

Ⓑ The pandas

Ⓒ The snakes

Ⓓ The seals

11. According to the map, which is located at (6,10)?

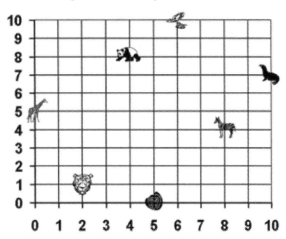

Ⓐ The seals

Ⓑ The monkeys

Ⓒ The snakes

Ⓓ The zebras

12. According to the map, what is the distance (along the grid) from the pandas ( ) to the monkeys ( ) ?

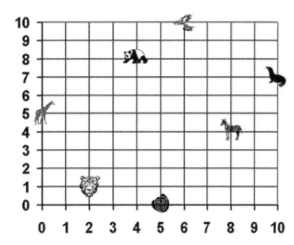

Ⓐ 9 units
Ⓑ 8 units
Ⓒ 1 unit
Ⓓ 6 units

13. **Which set of directions would lead a person from the giraffes (** **) to the tigers (** **)?**

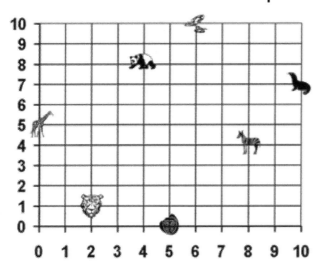

Ⓐ Walk 4 units along the x-axis and 2 units along the y-axis.
Ⓑ Walk 1 unit along the x-axis and 2 units along the y-axis.
Ⓒ Walk 2 units along the x-axis and 4 units along the y-axis.
Ⓓ Walk 4 units along the x-axis and 1 unit along the y-axis.

14. **Which would be the best location for the antelopes, so they are as far as possible from the tigers (** 🐯 **)?**

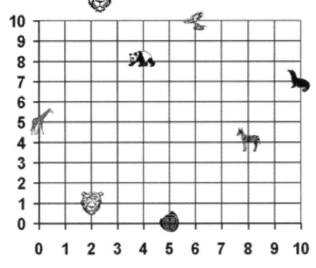

Ⓐ (3,3)
Ⓑ (0,4)
Ⓒ (6,1)
Ⓓ (8,8)

15. The graph below shows the total purchase price of game tickets depending on the amount of tickets purchased.

Based on this graph, what is the total cost for twelve tickets? Circle the correct answer choice.

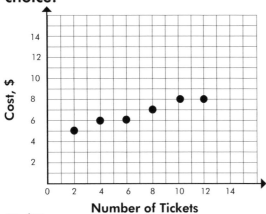

Ⓐ $5
Ⓑ $6
Ⓒ $7
Ⓓ $8

16. During her run, Liu records the number of minutes it took to reach six mile markers. Based on this graph determine if the statements below are true or false.

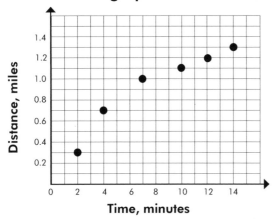

	True	False
Lui reaches mile marker 1.0 in seven minutes.	○	○
It took Lui two minutes to run from mile marker 1.0 to mile marker 1.2.	○	○
Lui ran from mile marker 1.1 to mail marker 1.2 in three minutes.	○	○
Fourteen minutes after Lui started she reached mile marker 1.3.	○	○

17. The weather station is at the coordinates (9,2).
   Plot the coordinate on the graph.

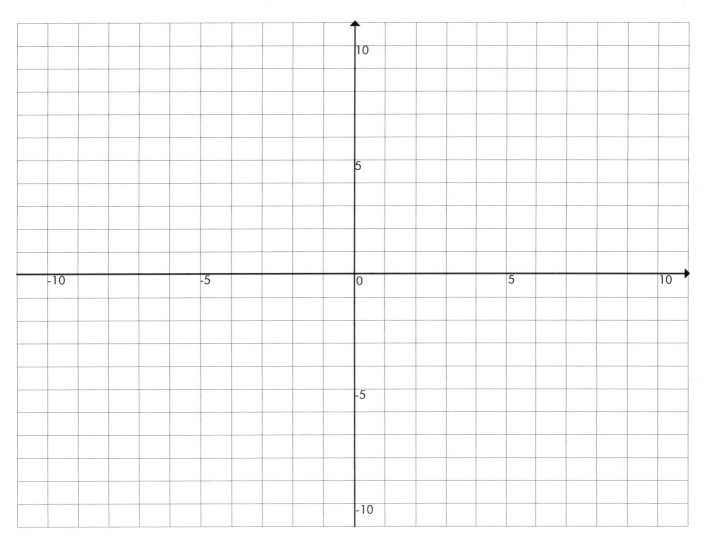

Chapter 6

Lesson 3: Properties of 2D Shapes

You can scan the QR code given below or use the url to access additional EdSearch resources including videos and mobile apps related to *Properties of 2D Shapes*.

Properties of 2D Shapes

URL	QR Code
http://www.lumoslearning.com/a/5gb3	

1. **Complete the following.**
   A plane figure is regular only if it has _____.

   Ⓐ equal sides
   Ⓑ congruent angles
   Ⓒ equal sides and congruent angles
   Ⓓ equal sides, congruent angles, and interior angles that total 180

2. **Complete the following.**
   Two _____ will always be similar.

   Ⓐ circles
   Ⓑ squares
   Ⓒ equilateral triangles
   Ⓓ all of the above

3. **Two interior angles of a triangle measure 30 degrees and 50 degrees. Which type of triangle could it be?**

   Ⓐ a right triangle
   Ⓑ an acute triangle
   Ⓒ an obtuse triangle
   Ⓓ an isosceles triangle

4. **Complete the following.**
   An angle measuring between 0 and 90 degrees is called a(n) _____.

   Ⓐ acute angle
   Ⓑ obtuse angle
   Ⓒ straight angle
   Ⓓ reflex angle

5. **Which of these is not a characteristic of a polygon?**

   Ⓐ a closed shape
   Ⓑ parallel faces
   Ⓒ made of straight lines
   Ⓓ two-dimensional

6. Complete the following.
   This isosceles triangle has _____.

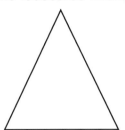

   Ⓐ one line of symmetry
   Ⓑ two congruent angles
   Ⓒ two equal sides
   Ⓓ all of the above

7. Marcus used tape and drinking straws to build the outline of a two-dimensional shape. He used four straws in all. Exactly three of the straws were of equal length. What might Marcus have built?

   Ⓐ a square
   Ⓑ a trapezoid
   Ⓒ a rectangle
   Ⓓ a rhombus

8. How many pairs of parallel sides does a regular octagon have?

   Ⓐ 8
   Ⓑ 4
   Ⓒ 2
   Ⓓ 0

9. A rectangle can be described by all of the following terms except _____.

   Ⓐ a parallelogram
   Ⓑ a polygon
   Ⓒ a prism
   Ⓓ a quadrilateral

10. Which of the following statements is not true?

    Ⓐ An equilateral triangle must have exactly 3 lines of symmetry.
    Ⓑ An equilateral triangle will have at least one 60-degree angle.
    Ⓒ An equilateral triangle must have rotational symmetry.
    Ⓓ All equilateral triangles are congruent.

11. Which of the following shapes is not a polygon?

Ⓐ semicircle
Ⓑ trapezoid
Ⓒ hexagon
Ⓓ decagon

12. What is the name for a polygon that has an acute exterior angle?

Ⓐ convex
Ⓑ concave
Ⓒ complex
Ⓓ simple

13. How many diagonals does a rectangle have?

Ⓐ 1
Ⓑ 2
Ⓒ 3
Ⓓ 4

14. Which shape is a polygon, a quadrilateral, and a rhombus?

Ⓐ an isosceles triangle
Ⓑ a rectangle
Ⓒ a square
Ⓓ a trapezoid

15. Which of the following terms does not describe a trapezoid?

Ⓐ a parallelogram
Ⓑ a polygon
Ⓒ a quadrilateral
Ⓓ a quadrangle

16. Read the statements below and indicate whether they are true or false.

	True	False
All squares are rhombuses.	◯	◯
All parallelograms have four right angles.	◯	◯
All trapezoids have at least one set of parallel sides.	◯	◯
All squares are rectangles.	◯	◯

17. Circle the word below that describes all trapezoids.

Ⓐ   Parallelogram

Ⓑ   Rhombus

Ⓒ   Square

Ⓓ   Quadrilateral

Chapter 6

Lesson 4: Classifying 2D Shapes

You can scan the QR code given below or use the url to access additional EdSearch resources including videos and mobile apps related to *Classifying 2D Shapes*.

 **Classifying 2D Shapes**

URL	QR Code
http://www.lumoslearning.com/a/5gb4	

1. **Which shape belongs in the center of the diagram?**

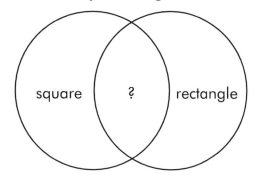

   Ⓐ triangle
   Ⓑ circle
   Ⓒ square
   Ⓓ polygon

2. **Which shape belongs in section B of the diagram?**

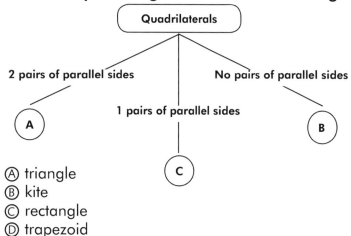

   Ⓐ triangle
   Ⓑ kite
   Ⓒ rectangle
   Ⓓ trapezoid

3. **Which shape belongs in section C of the diagram?**

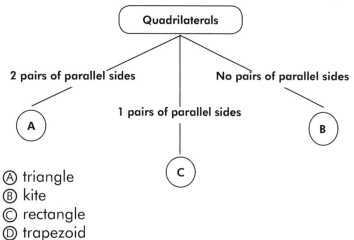

   Ⓐ triangle
   Ⓑ kite
   Ⓒ rectangle
   Ⓓ trapezoid

4. **Which shape does not belong in section A of the diagram?**

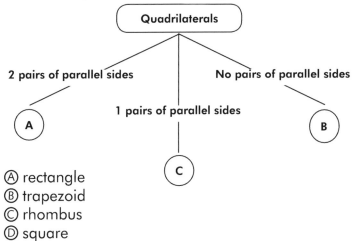

Ⓐ rectangle
Ⓑ trapezoid
Ⓒ rhombus
Ⓓ square

5. **Which shape belongs in section A of the diagram?**

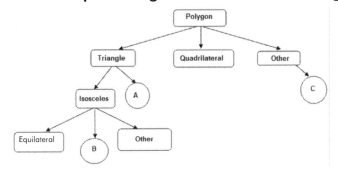

Ⓐ scalene
Ⓑ right
Ⓒ acute
Ⓓ symmetrical

6. **Which shape belongs in section B of the diagram?**

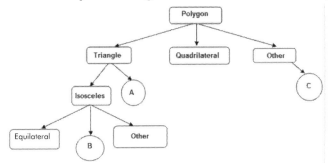

Ⓐ Scalene
Ⓑ Isosceles Right
Ⓒ Acute
Ⓓ Symmetrical

7. **Which shape does not belong in section C of the diagram?**

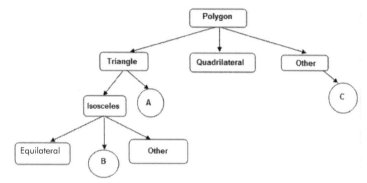

Ⓐ Octagon
Ⓑ Decagon
Ⓒ Pentagon
Ⓓ Rhombus

8. **Which statement is true?**

Ⓐ All triangles are quadrangles.
Ⓑ All polygons are hexagons.
Ⓒ All parallelograms are polygons.
Ⓓ All parallelograms are rectangles.

9. **Which statement is false?**

Ⓐ All octagons are parallelograms.
Ⓑ All rectangles are quadrangles.
Ⓒ All triangles are polygons.
Ⓓ All rectangles are quadrilaterals.

10. **Which statement defines a quadrangle?**

Ⓐ Any rectangle that has 4 sides of equal length
Ⓑ Any quadrilateral with 2 pairs of parallel sides
Ⓒ Any polygon with 4 angles
Ⓓ Any polygon with 4 or more sides

11. Which shape is a quadrilateral but not a parallelogram?

Ⓐ

Ⓑ

Ⓒ

Ⓓ

12. Which shape is a rhombus but not a square?

Ⓐ

Ⓑ

Ⓒ

Ⓓ

13. In a hierarchy of shapes, how could the category of "pentagon" be split in two?

Ⓐ polygon and non-polygon
Ⓑ 5 sides and 6 sides
Ⓒ parallelogram and not parallelogram
Ⓓ regular and non-regular

14. Which triangle would be classified as equiangular?

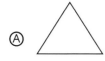

Ⓐ

Ⓑ

Ⓒ

Ⓓ

15. Which shape would not be classified as regular?

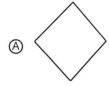

Ⓐ

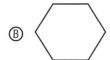

Ⓑ

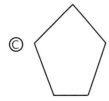

Ⓒ

Ⓓ

16. Circle the shape that is a parallelogram with four equal sides and one of the angles measuring 55 degrees

Ⓐ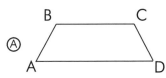

Ⓑ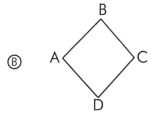

Ⓒ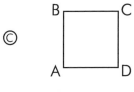

Ⓓ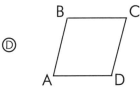

17. Which of the following quadrilaterals has all the properties listed below?

· At least one pair of parallel sides.

· Opposites sides are equal.

· All sides are congruent.

· Not all angles are equal.

Ⓐ Rhombus
Ⓑ Trapezoid
Ⓒ Rectangle
Ⓓ Square

End of Geometry

Chapter 6: Geometry

Answer Key
&
Detailed Explanations

Lesson 1: Coordinate Geometry

Question No.	Answer	Detailed Explanations
1	C	A rectangle must have two pairs of parallel sides, so point D must be at 2 on the x-axis (in line with point A) and at 0 on the y-axis (in line with point C).
2	B	Segment AB (from 2 to 5) is 3 units long. Segment BC (from 0 to 4) is 4 units long. Segment BC is longer.
3	B	Using the labels, follow the x-axis as far as point R (7 units) and the y-axis as far as point R (2 units). This makes the coordinate pair (7, 2).
4	D	To find point (4, 3), follow the x-axis horizontally 4 units, then follow the y-axis vertically 3 units. The result is point O.
5	A	Using the labels, follow the x-axis as far as point P (5 units) and the y-axis as far as point P (5 units). This makes the coordinate pair (5, 5).
6	C	The coordinate pair is (c, 4), so follow the line on the graph to where its value for y is 4. Follow that point down to the x-axis to see it is 6.
7	B	The coordinate pair is (2, b), so follow the line on the graph to where its value for x is 2. Follow that point across to the y-axis to see it is 2.
8	B	As the value of x increases, the value of y increases equally. This produces an upward-sloping straight line.
9	A	The origin is point (0, 0). The point closest to this would have the lowest x- and y- values (without being negative numbers).
10	B	The points would create this diamond: The top of the diamond is point (5, 8).

Question No.	Answer	Detailed Explanations
11	D	When the four points are plotted and connected, they form this polygon: It is a trapezoid.
12	C	Option (A) in equation form becomes $y = 1 + x$. (8, 5) does not satisfies this equation [even though (0, 1) satisfies this equation]. Option (B) in equation form becomes $y = 2x$. (0, 1) does not satisfy this equation. Option (D) in equation form becomes $y = 1 + 2x$. (8, 5) does not satisfy this equation [even though (0, 1) satisfies this equation]. Option (C) in equation form becomes $y = x/2 + 1$. Both the known points (0, 1) and (8, 5) satisfy this equation. Therefore option (C) is correct.
13	D	Naming point (3, 4) point L would make segment LO parallel to segment PQ, and it would make segment LP parallel to segment OQ.
14	C	In this example, one value for x has three different values for y. This will create a straight vertical line.

Question No.	Answer	Detailed Explanations
15	A	The functions would create these two intersecting lines:

Question No.	Answer	Detailed Explanations
16	C	The x-axis is the horizontal line in a coordinate grid and is represented by the letter T in the picture.
17	C	Each point has coordinates (x-coordinate, y-coordinate). To determine the coordinates for each point, first determine the x-coordinate of the point and then the y-coordinate of the point. Be very careful to notice the interval of each division of the grid.

This grid has a y-axis that increases by one for each division. The x-axis, however, increases by 2 for each division.

Point A has an x-coordinate of 4 and a y-coordinate of 6 or (4,6).

Point B has an x-coordinate of 18 and a y-coordinate of 5 or (18,5).

Point C has an x-coordinate of 12 and a y-coordinate of 10 or (12,10).

The correct answer choice is C.

Lesson 2: Real World Graphing Problems

Question No.	Answer	Detailed Explanations
1	C	The location of the weather station is at the intersection of 9 on the x-axis and 2 on the y-axis. Therefore, its coordinates are (9,2).
2	B	The location of the warehouse is at the intersection of 0 on the x-axis and 4 on the y-axis. Therefore, its coordinates are (0,4).
3	A	At the intersection of 7 on the x-axis and 2 on the y-axis, the hospital is located.
4	B	At the intersection of 5 on the x-axis and 5 on the y-axis, the bridge is located.
5	D	Starting at the playground (2,9), walking 7 units along the -ve y-axis could bring a person to (2,2). From there, walking 5 units along the +ve x-axis could bring that person to (7,2), to the location of the hospital.
6	C	Starting at the weather station (9,2), walking 4 units along the -ve x-axis could bring a person to (5,2). From there, walking 3 units along the +ve y-axis could bring that person to (5,5), to the location of the bridge.
7	B	This is the only set of coordinates given that is located between the warehouse and the hospital, making it the closest to both locations.
8	A	The location of the zebras is at the intersection of 8 on the x-axis and 4 on the y-axis. Therefore, its coordinates are (8,4).
9	B	The location of the giraffes is at the intersection of 0 on the x-axis and 5 on the y-axis. Therefore, its coordinates are (0,5).
10	D	At the intersection of 10 on the x-axis and 7 on the y-axis, the seals are located.
11	C	At the intersection of 6 on the x-axis and 10 on the y-axis, the snakes are located.
12	A	The pandas are located at 8 on the y-axis and the monkeys are located at 0 on the y-axis. The difference is 8 units. The pandas are located at 4 on the x-axis and the monkeys are located at 5 on the x-axis. The difference is 1 unit. All together, the distance is 9 units (8 + 1 = 9).
13	C	Starting at the giraffes (0,5), walking 2 units along the x-axis could bring a person to (2,5). From there, walking 4 units along the y-axis could bring that person to (2,1), the location of the tigers.
14	D	This is the furthest location from the tigers, which are located at (2,1).

Question No.	Answer	Detailed Explanations
15	D	The last point represents twelve tickets. Since the y-coordinate is $8, this means that twelve tickets cost $8. The correct answer is D.

16			True	False
	Lui reaches mile marker 1.0 in seven minutes. The x-coordinate associated with y = 1.0 is 7.		●	○
	It took Lui two minutes to run from mile marker 1.0 to mile marker 1.2. Lui was at mile marker 1.0 at 7 minutes. She reached mile marker 1.2 at 12 minutes. Thus it took her 12-7 = 5 minutes to run from mile marker 1.0 to 1.2.		○	●
	Lui ran from mile marker 1.1 to mail marker 1.2 in three minutes. Lui was at mile marker 1.1 at 10 minutes. She reached mile marker 1.2 at 12 minutes. Thus it took her 12-10 = 2 minutes to run from mile marker 1.1 to 1.2.		○	●
	Fourteen minutes after Lui started she reached mile marker 1.3. The y-coordinate associated with x = 14 is 1.3.		●	○

Question No.	Answer	Detailed Explanations
17		The coordinates (9,2) shows 9 points on x axis and 2 on y axis. Count the number of points on each axis and mark it.

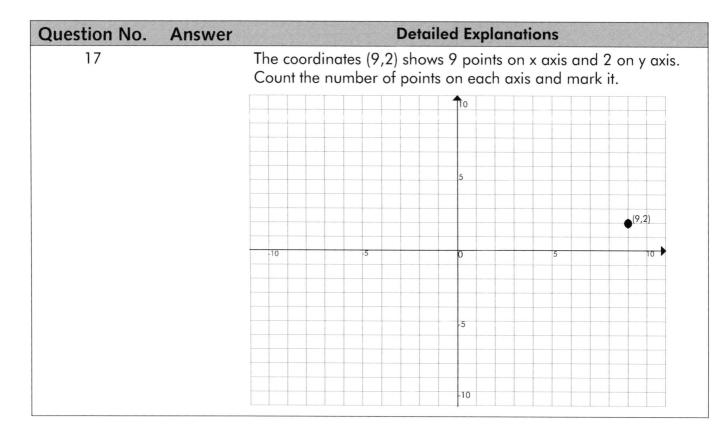

Lesson 3: Properties of 2D Shapes

Question No.	Answer	Detailed Explanations
1	C	In a regular plane figure, all sides are equal lengths and all angles are congruent. However the angles do not have to total 180.
2	D	Similar shapes do not have to be the same size, but they must be the same shape. All sides must have the same ratio. Since circles, squares, and equilateral triangles always have the same ratio of sides (or dimension, in the case of the circle), they are always similar.
3	C	Remember that the three interior angles of a triangle always equal 180 degrees. If two of the angles equal 80 degrees, the third angle must be 100 degrees. Any triangle with an angle greater than 90 degrees is obtuse.
4	A	An acute angle is less than 90 degrees.
5	B	Since polygons are two-dimensional, they do not have faces.
6	D	By definition, an isosceles triangle has two equal sides and two congruent angles. It also has one line of symmetry (in this model, a vertical line through the center).
7	B	Marcus could not have made a square or a rhombus since only three of the sides were of equal length. He also could not have made a rectangle, since the number of equal sides on a rectangle is either 2 or 4 (if it is a square). The shape he made must have been an (isosceles) trapezoid.
8	B	All of the opposite sides of a regular octagon are parallel. Since there are 8 sides, there are 4 pairs.
9	C	A prism is a 3-dimensional shape. Even though it can consist of rectangular faces, a rectangle is not a prism.
10	D	In order to be congruent, all equilateral triangles would have to be the same size, which they are not. Equilateral triangles of any size do have 3 lines of symmetry, 3 60-degree angles, and rotational symmetry.
11	A	A polygon is a closed 2-dimensional figure that is made entirely of straight lines. Since a semicircle has a curved side, it is not a polygon.
12	B	A concave polygon has at least one exterior angle that is acute (or one interior angle that is obtuse).
13	B	A diagonal is a straight line that connects one corner of a polygon with another corner (but is not a side). All quadrilaterals have two diagonals.

Question No.	Answer	Detailed Explanations
14	C	While it is a polygon and a quadrilateral, it is the fact that it is a rhombus (4 equal-length sides) that makes this figure a square.
15	A	A trapezoid is a flat, closed figure made of straight lines (a polygon). It has four sides (a quadrilateral) and four angles (a quadrangle). It has only one set of opposite sides parallel, so it is not a parallelogram (two pairs of parallel sides).

16

	True	False
All squares are rhombuses.	⦿	○
All parallelograms have four right angles.	○	⦿
All trapezoids have at least one set of parallel sides.	⦿	○
All squares are rectangles.	⦿	○

(1) Since all sides of a square are equal, a square is also a rhombus. Therefore, the 1st statement is true.

(2) All parallelograms need not have four right angles. Therefore, the 2nd statement is false.

(3) A trapezoid has only one pair of parallel lines. Therefore, the 3rd statement is true.

(4) Each angle of a square measures 90 degrees. So, every square is also a rectangle. Therefore, the 4th statement is true.

| 17 | D | Answer D is the right choice. |

Lesson 4: Classifying 2D Shapes

Question No.	Answer	Detailed Explanations
1	C	A square is both a rhombus and a rectangle.
2	D	A trapezoid is a quadrilateral with one pair of parallel sides.
3	B	A kite is a quadrilateral with no pairs of parallel sides.
4	B	A trapezoid is a quadrilateral which has only one pair of parallel sides.
5	A	Scalene is a type of triangle that is not isosceles.
6	B	An isosceles triangle can also be a right triangle (one with a 90° angle). Then it is called an isosceles right triangle.
7	D	A rhombus has four sides, so it would fall under the heading quadrilateral in the hierarchy.
8	C	A polygon is a closed 2-dimensional figure made up of straight lines. Therefore, all parallelograms are polygons.
9	A	An octagon is any 8-sided polygon. Parallelograms have 4 sides.
10	C	A quadrangle is simply any closed 2-dimensional figure made up of straight lines (a polygon) that has 4 sides or 4 angles. Options A and B fall under the classification of quadrangle, but they do not define it entirely.
11	B	The trapezoid is a quadrilateral because it has four sides, but it is not a parallelogram because it does not have 2 sets of parallel sides.
12	D	Figure shown in option (D) is a rhombus because it is a parallelogram with 4 sides of equal length, but it is not a square because it does not have 4 right angles. Figure shown in option (B) is a rhombus. But it is also a square.
13	D	A pentagon can be either regular (having all sides and angles the same) or non-regular (having 5 sides and angles that differ).
14	A	An equiangular triangle is one in which all three angles are equal (also called an equilateral triangle because the three sides are the same length).
15	C	A regular polygon is one in which all angles are the same and all sides are the same length. This pentagon has sides and angles that differ.

Question No.	Answer	Detailed Explanations
16	B	A rhombus and a square are both parallelograms with four equal sides. The square, however, has equal angles (90degrees each). Therefore the correct answer is 'B' the rhombus.
17	A	The correct answer is A.

In row 16, the following figure appears:

B

A   C

D

SBAC FAQ

What will SBAC Math Assessments Look Like?

In many ways, the SBAC assessments will be unlike anything many students have ever seen. The tests will be conducted online, requiring students complete tasks to assess a deeper understanding of the CCSS. The students will be assessed once 75% of the year has been completed in two different assessments - a Computer Adaptive Testing (CAT) and a Performance Task (PT).

The time for each Math portion is described below:

Estimated Time on Task in Minutes		
Grade	CAT	PT
3	90	60
4	90	60
5	90	60
6	120	60
7	120	60
8	120	60

Because the assessment is online, the test will consist of a combination of new types of questions:

1. Drag and Drop
2. Drop Down
3. Essay Response
4. Extended Constructed Response
5. Hot Text Select and Drag
6. Hot Text Selective Highlight
7. Matching Table In-line
8. Matching Table Single Response
9. Multiple Choice – Single Correct Response, radial buttons
10. Multiple Choice – Multiple Response, check boxes
11. Numeric Response
12. Short Text
13. Table Fill-in

For more information on 2022-23 Assessment year, visit
www.lumoslearning.com/a/sbac-2022-faqs OR
Scan the **QR Code**

What is this SBAC Test Practice Book?

Inside this book, you will find practice sections aligned to each CCSS. Students will have the ability to review questions on each standard, one section at a time, in the order presented, or they can choose to study the sections where they need the most practice.

In addition to the practice sections, you will have access to two full-length CAT and PT practice tests online. Completing these tests will help students master the different areas that are included in newly aligned SBAC tests and practice test taking skills. The results will help the students and educators get insights into students' strengths and weaknesses in specific content areas. These insights could be used to help students strengthen their skills in difficult topics and to improve speed and accuracy while taking the test.

Because the SBAC assessment includes newly created, technology-enhanced questions, it is necessary for students to be able to regularly practice these questions. The Lumos online StepUp program includes thirteen technology enhanced questions that mimic the types students will see during the assessments.

Discover Engaging and Relevant Learning Resources

Lumos EdSearch is a safe search engine specifically designed for teachers and students. Using EdSearch, you can easily find thousands of standards-aligned learning resources such as questions, videos, lessons, worksheets and apps. Teachers can use EdSearch to create custom resource kits to perfectly match their lesson objective and assign them to one or more students in their classroom.

To access the EdSearch tool, use the search box after you log into Lumos StepUp or use the link provided below.

www.lumoslearning.com/a/edsearchb

The Lumos Standards Coherence map provides information about previous level, next level and related standards. It helps educators and students visually explore learning standards. It's an effective tool to help students progress through the learning objectives. Teachers can use this tool to develop their own pacing charts and lesson plans. Educators can also use the coherence map to get deep insights into why a student is struggling in a specific learning objective.

Teachers can access the Coherence maps after logging into the StepUp Teacher Portal or use the link provided below.

www.lumoslearning.com/a/coherence-map

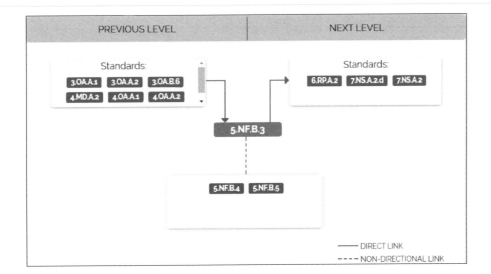

Progress Chart

Standard	Lesson	Page No.	Practice		Mastered	Re-practice /Reteach
CCSS			Date	Score		
5.OA.A.1	Write & Interpret Numerical Expressions & Patterns	9				
5.OA.A.2	Record and Interpret Calculations with Numbers	12				
5.OA.B.3	Analyze Patterns and Relationships	15				
5.NBT.A.1	Place Value	31				
5.NBT.A.2	Multiplication & Division of Powers of Ten	35				
5.NBT.A.3.	Read and Write Decimals	39				
5.NBT.A.3.	Comparing and Ordering Decimals	43				
5.NBT.A.4	Rounding Decimals	47				
5.NBT.B.5	Multiplication of Whole Numbers	51				
5.NBT.B.6	Division of Whole Numbers	55				
5.NBT.B.7	Add, Subtract, Multiply, and Divide Decimals	59				
5.NF.A.1	Add & Subtract Fractions	90				
5.NF.A.2	Problem Solving with Fractions	96				
5.NF.B.3	Interpreting Fractions	101				
5.NF.B.4	Multiply Fractions	105				
5.NF.B.4.B	Multiply to Find Area	110				
5.NF.B.5.A	Multiplication as Scaling	115				
5.NF.B.5.B	Numbers Multiplied by Fractions	119				
5.NF.B.6	Real World Problems with Fractions	123				
5.NF.B.7.A	Dividing Fractions	128				
5.NF.B.7.B	Dividing by Unit Fractions	132				
5.NF.B.7.C	Real World Problems Dividing Fractions	136				

Standard	Lesson	Page No.	Practice		Mastered	Re-practice /Reteach
CCSS			Date	Score		
5.MD.A.1	Converting Units of Measure	170				
5.MD.B.2	Representing and Interpreting Data	174				
5.MD.C.3.A	Volume	190				
5.MD.C.3.B	Cubic Units	195				
5.MD.C.4	Counting Cubic Units	199				
5.MD.C.5.A	Multiply to Find Volume	204				
5.MD.C.5.B	Real World Problems with Volume	208				
5.MD.C.5.C	Adding Volumes	212				
5.G.A.1	Coordinate Geometry	231				
5.G.A.2	Real World Graphing Problems	240				
5.G.B.3	Properties of 2D Shapes	250				
5.G.B.4	Classifying 2D Shapes	255				

Grade 5

SBAC Practice
ENGLISH
LANGUAGE ARTS LITERACY
Test Prep

UPDATED for 2022-23
Smarter Balanced Study Guide

2 Performance Tasks (PT)

2 Computer Adaptive Tests (CAT)

COVERS 40+ SKILLS

Smarter Balanced Assessment Consortium, which does not sponsor or endorse this product.

Available

• At Leading book stores

• Online www.LumosLearning.com